Being able to communicate the complexities of love is a gift, and few are as gifted at this as Chris DuPré. His ability to unfold and unpack the many layers and meanings of love is amazing. In *The Love Project*, Chris offers insight and understanding that is new, profound, and will impact the way you look at and communicate love.

MICHAEL W. SMITH
Singer/Songwriter

Too often we stop at *I love you*. Far too often we don't have the right words to convey the unique qualities we see and love in someone. This heartfelt book by Chris DuPré gives you examples of how to express your love in genuine, life-giving ways that are practical, simple, and honest. *The Love Project* will not only inspire you, it will change you as well as those around you. I absolutely love this book!

MELODY GREEN
Melody Green Ministries
Cofounder of Last Days Ministries

A physician once said, "The best medicine for humans is love." Someone asked, "What if it doesn't work?" The physician smiled and said, "Increase the dose." In *The Love Project*, Chris DuPré gives you practical advice on how to increase the dose. This is your guide to living loved and changing the world around you.

GORDON ROBERTSON
CEO, The Christian Broadcasting Network

Chris DuPré has written about a subject that he knows very well… love. If you want to know what's in a man, don't just listen to him; listen to those around him. I've known Chris for almost twenty-five years and he is one of the most loved men I know. That just doesn't happen in a vacuum. It's because Chris knows something about how to love others well. *The Love Project* is the fruit of his many years of giving time and attention to all who come across his path. His reputation as a "father" to those around him is legendary. You would be well served to take hold of this book and glean all you can from it. It has within its pages the potential to change your life and to also change the world around you.

MIKE BICKLE
Founder and Director of the
International House of Prayer Missions Base of Kansas City

When talking about the ways of God, love reigns supreme. Chris not only knows the ways of God, but he personifies them. In *The Love Project*, through his characteristic lens of humor and a father's heart, Chris shows us who we are in God and how we can become more of who we are meant to be. He makes the accurate observation that we tend to live out of the things we have experienced, but then he invites us to experience life in the atmosphere of God and to live out of the identity of the child who is perfectly and fully loved.

BROWN BANNISTER
Grammy and Dove Award–winning Producer and Songwriter

The Love Project. What a title! And what an amazing theme! Chris hits the central issue in all of life. His writing is poetic, articulate, and philosophical, yet reaches deeply into the heart of human need and desire. You must read this book! It will help you understand life, yourself, and your purpose for being here. Chris rightly points out that "The Love Project" started in heaven.

JOHN ARNOTT
Catch the Fire/Partners in Harvest, Toronto

This world is desperately awaiting the one convincing proof that is needed—the simple power of love unleashed. *The Love Project* is a trumpet call awakening us to that very thing.

BRAD CUMMINGS
Coauthor, Publisher, and Film Producer of *The Shack*

We've known Chris DuPré for nearly a quarter century and have been pleasantly jarred by his unique ability to affirm us and clearly voice his love for us in very specific ways. It's not how we commonly speak to one another in this busy world. After reading *The Love Project*, we now see the why behind the what of Chris' practical expressions of love. Whether it's friendship, workplace, ministry, marriage, or family, Chris challenges each of us to give voice to our love for others in practical, meaningful ways that can change lives. Thank you, Chris, for your friendship and thank you for challenging us to love others more extravagantly as we initiate our own love project.

STEVE AND JANE LAMBERT
Creators and Publishers of *Five in a Row*

I've been blessed to be Chris's friend since elementary school. If there ever was a modern-day David-and-Jonathan relationship, it is ours! Thanks for writing and living *The Love Project*, and for encouraging us all to be more intentional in our love for one another.

TOM SPITTAL
Senior Director, Global Compliance, AstraZeneca

As you read *The Love Project*, you will discover that it is the gift that keeps on giving. As I was scanning it for a quick overview by myself, I got caught up and started reading every word to my wife Barbara, blurting out at intervals, "That's really great." Chris clarifies often-heard, familiar Scriptures with passion. There were also intervals of crying, laughing, and healing of my own heart. I told my wife, "This book is like an emotional GPS, the Lord pointing us in the right direction." I've had the privilege to know Chris for over twenty years and I can say that he is the real deal. Out of the abundance of the heart the mouth speaks.

MICKEY ROBINSON
Author, International Speaker

There is a lot of God (i.e., Love) in Chris DuPré. I first met him when he was the worship leader at Catch the Fire Toronto. The positive impact of his worship leading and his heart so full of God are still being felt here. Chris's first book, *The Wild Love of God*, was a revelation of our Father's love for us and impacted my life significantly. *The Love Project* carries that story on, not just for us, but for all those around us. Our church's motto is this: *To Receive God's Love and Give It Away to Toronto and the World*. Chris got a download of the manual on how to do that and he wrote it down for all of us. I can't see how you won't be blessed by this book.

MICHAEL MANFORD
Chairman, Strategic Market Research Inc.
Toronto, Canada

In *The Love Project*, Chris DuPré has generated a culturally relevant and kingdom-minded message. In a time when the definitions of love are mixed up, and in many cases love is almost totally lacking, this is a most profound and timely book. Chris is one who lives the message of intentional affection. Therefore, as he lives it, he can give it. Now we need to get it, read it, and live it!

SCOTT MACLEOD
Author, Producer, Musician, International Speaker
President and Founder of Provision International

I have had the honor of knowing Chris DuPré and his amazing family since 1997. I personally know that the first four words Chris writes in this book are a true statement! He loves ice cream; however, he loves people most. He loves people well. I have witnessed firsthand as Chris lived each of the chapters in this book. I have heard him speak these very paragraphs. Every word on every page is merely an overflow of his life as a husband, son, father, friend, and lover of God. I can think of no better person than Chris DuPré to write *The Love Project*, because he did not simply write about it; he has lived this way for years, and we get to glean gold nuggets from someone who makes it of great importance to love people well. In the age of social media where people rarely look each other in the eye as meetings, conversations, and conflict are more and more handled through e-mail, it is a crucial word straight from the heart of God for these days.

JULIE MEYER
Julie Meyer Ministries
International House Of Prayer–KC

THE Love PROJECT

CHRIS DUPRÉ

BroadStreet
PUBLISHING

BroadStreet Publishing Group
Racine, Wisconsin, USA
www.broadstreetpublishing.com

ISBN-13: 9781424549153 (hard cover)
ISBN-13: 9781424550067 (e-book)

Cover design by Chris Garborg at www.garborgdesign.com
Typesetting by Katherine Lloyd at www.TheDESKonline.com

Stock or custom editions of BroadStreet Publishing titles may be purchased in bulk for educational, business, ministry, fundraising, or sales promotional use. For information, please e-mail info@broadstreetpublishing.com.

Printed in China

Writing a book about love doesn't come along every day. So when it comes to doing a dedication for a book on this subject, there is only one person at the top of my list: my wife, Laura DuPré.

She is the most amazing woman I have ever known. Her love for me, our children, and our grandchildren is fierce, unyielding, and boundless. I have become better as a person and a man as a result of being married to her. May every reader understand that the subject of love within these pages has been enhanced and magnified because of my wife. She is my coauthor. So, to you, Laura, I dedicate this book. Thank you for loving me so well all these years.

Contents

INTRODUCTION

I love ice cream. I'm not a coffee drinker, so that flavor doesn't thrill me, but bring on the chocolate, vanilla (with chocolate syrup), or strawberry (also with chocolate syrup). Don't forget the sherbet and gelato, too, and please, please don't forget the frozen custard—Abbott's Frozen Custard from Rochester, New York. Oh, yeah!

I love a good movie. I've loved movies since I was a kid, and even today a good movie will transport me to a place of laughter, peace, suspense, or even to a place of greater understanding.

I love music. From the moment I could walk I've been embarrassing everyone around me (especially my kids) as I "move" to the music. When the Beatles were on *Ed Sullivan* in February of 1964, it cemented my love for music. When I was growing up, our home was filled with everything from Mario Lanza to old Broadway tunes to the latest rock-and-roll songs.

I love spring. When winter drops its icy hold on the cold

and darkness, it's such a joy to feel the increased warmth and light and to know that more days like that are on the way.

I love… I love… I love…

I could go on all day about the things I love. My wife, my kids, my grandchildren, my friends, even the places I've been and the many experiences I've gone through.

Life is about loving. It's why we're here. We were created to be loved so that we can, in turn, love others. Did you hear that? Just to make sure, let me say it again. We were created for the purpose of being loved so that, in turn, we may love others.

I went for years without losing a loved one. Then, within a short period of time, I suffered the loss of three of the dearest people in my life. In 1990 I lost my grandmother (the only grandparent I ever knew, who was like a second mother), in 1991 my father suddenly passed away, and in 1992 my mother passed away after a very short illness. My grandmother's passing was expected—she was ninety-nine. But my parents were in their mid-sixties, and their deaths were both sudden and unexpected.

In the months after their deaths, I occasionally found myself about to give one of them a call to tell them about something that was happening with me or with one of my kids. Then I would realize that they were no longer there. I couldn't call them, nor would I see them soon at some family function. Time had continued to move ahead, and during its journey, time ushered people—people I loved—into their eternal home.

Though I realize that I can no longer tell them the things I want to say, I am mindful that I am surrounded by people I know and love, still on this side of death's door, which reminds me that it's not too late to say the things that need to be said. It's not too late for them.

A few years ago a young man walked by me in church and said, "Love ya, man. Call me." It would have been innocent enough, but I was a father figure to him and I hadn't seen him in over a year. I realized that he was in a hurry, and getting anything from him that day was great, so I smiled and waved back.

My antenna went up after that moment and I have become very aware of how shallow we are with our words of praise, encouragement, and affirmation. Even the phrase "I love you" lacks the power it is meant to have. "I love ice cream, I love the NFL, and I love you." Well, thanks.

> "I love you" is good, but "I love you because..." is better. The ability to express our love and appreciation for one another, with specifics, is crucial.

We live in a world of comparison and competition, yet God made us all different. So often we can't see the beauty within us, yet others see it clearly. We need to call out those things we see in each other and to share, bless, and help transform their perspectives so that they are not just seeing what others see, but they begin to see themselves as God sees them.

So I think it's time for a revolution. It's time for a love movement! From books to songs to TV and movies, it's time we awakened the world to life's most important subject: love. *The Love Boat* may have sailed away a long time ago, but to God, because His very nature is love, it's time to once again get on board and sail into His ocean of affection. I know, that last sentence was a bit flowery, maybe even corny, but I like it.

As we begin this journey together, I want to say that I am not the expert on what it means to love. Jesus is. I am, like you, on my own journey to discover what it means to love as He loves. Looking at the state our world is in, I believe it's time to fill the airways with the reality of the power of love. It's time for a national conversation on the benefits of loving one another in real and practical ways— at home, at work, with family, friends, and even strangers. It's time for a movement based on living lives of intentional affection. It's time for *The Love Project*.

1

THE LOOK OF LOVE

L ove. We all want it. We all need it. Without it, we are miserable. Is it any wonder why the world passionately pursues all things having to do with love?

Every culture leaves in its wake an image of what life was like and what was important and meaningful within that culture. One of the clearest ways we can see how love is thought of and expressed within our own culture is through TV, music, and movies.

As a young boy, I had my own world with friends, sports, and school, but I knew there was another world out there. I grew up in Upstate New York in a small town about twenty miles east of Rochester. It probably had as many cows as it did people. Cows don't sing and dance much. Because finances were slim, I was only able to experience the outside world through the lens of our little TV and our fold-down turntable. What I saw through that little lens was larger than life, and in the middle of it all came the same concept over and over. Love found, love enjoyed, new love, old love, love lost, love found again. Love was talked about, sung about, and played out in one scenario after another.

So it is today. Music is still filled with the overriding concept of love. In doing a search of the greatest songs of all time, you can't help but see that love is the central theme in almost all of them. Even the Beatles didn't do a song about another subject besides love for almost three years, when they finally put out the song "Nowhere Man" as a single in February 1966.

Looking at the list of the greatest love songs of all time, I am struck by how almost all of them have the same message. They talk about the power of love, letting your loved one know how wonderful she looks tonight, or knowing that someone loves you just the way you are. Song after song describes what every heart longs for: someone who loves me for who I am, and because of that, I finally have someone to love in return.

Think about the movie themes over the years. In *The Wizard of Oz*, Dorothy doesn't see the love that surrounds her. She is dreaming of a place over the rainbow where everything is perfect. Birds are singing, flowers are blooming, and all is right in the world. When, after a fierce storm, she is confronted with that seemingly ideal world, she quickly finds out it's not everything she thought it would be. There are witches, flying monkeys, and talking trees that slap your hands. That's nothing like what she grew up with in Kansas.

It doesn't take long in this new and strange world for her to feel deep within what she really longs for. Family. Home. Love. When all is stripped away, she realizes that Auntie Em's love is not a limiting love, it's a nurturing and caring love. In the movie we don't know anything about her parents. But if a young girl is living with her aunt and uncle, we can assume that something tragic happened to them, and therefore to her. With that in mind it's no wonder she was looking for something, anything, that could transport her out of her dull and hurting black-and-white world into a world filled with bright colors and all the positive fantasies she could imagine.

In the end love wins out. She must get home, and she is willing to do anything to get there—even take on that witch who wants her dead. When she awakens back in her black-and-white world, nothing there has changed. It's still black and white, and the same people are there. But one thing is different. She is. Her heart finally sees the affection in the hearts of those who have been by her side for years.

> When our hearts are awakened to love,
> everything changes.

From there let's jump to an old classic that was beautifully brought to the screen by Disney in 1991. *Beauty and the Beast* is all about love. An arrogant young prince is turned into a beast to teach him humility. And maybe, just maybe, if someone can fall in love with him in that beastly state, he will return to his old self in bodily form, hopefully keeping and growing in his newfound humility.

While watching this with my grandchildren, one of them said to me and my wife, "Hey, Papa and Bella, how was the beast changed back into a handsome prince?" My wife answered sweetly, "Well, honey, she loved his ugly parts away." After she said that, I looked at her and she looked at me and we both realized the power of those words. Wow! She loved his ugly parts away. That's the power of love!

From *You've Got Mail* to *Casablanca* to *Wall-E*, love is the driving force behind almost all movies. It's what people fight for, sacrifice all for, and in the end, it's what saves people.

Some of the most powerful expressions of love have nothing to do with romance. In the last twenty years there have been scores of movies that deal with the love, or lack thereof, between a father and his son. *Gladiator* is the story of a special love between a fatherlike figure and a man he welcomes into his life and home as if he were his child. His own son, filled with jealousy, becomes overwhelmed with hatred, and as a result, he is one of the screen's most all-time hated villains. When love is deeply desired and then rejected, it becomes a powerful weapon.

In the movie *Big Fish*, a dying father tells the story of his life as his jaded son listens. The young man has heard these stories time and again and is more embarrassed by his father than he is proud of him. But as the story progresses something happens to the son's heart. He moves from being detached to finally realizing that the truth of his father's stories is less important than the heart of the man himself. As his father lies there dying, he has one more chance to love him before it's too late. He comes to see the man his father really is, and we join him in a good cry as his life, and the movie, come to an end.

Speaking of tears, just try to see *Field of Dreams* for the first time (or the fourth or fifth) without shedding a tear. You don't know for sure how the protagonist's vision or dreams will be fulfilled or why he has to build a baseball field in the middle of his cornfield. Then, at the end, his father (or his ghost) shows up and you know. They walk toward each other and end up playing catch. Many men I know always lose it at that moment. A father and son's love restored means everything.

Even *Finding Nemo* had me smiling, with a lump in my throat, when the father finally found his son. By the way, if you haven't seen it, I'm sorry if I just ruined the ending for you. He found Nemo.

While I grew up loving movies, I believe my brother loves them more. The Academy Awards is his Super Bowl night. He graduated from Columbia University with such luminary titles as Phi Beta Kappa and magna cum laude. I, on the other hand, got a $250 scholarship from the Marion Jaycees when I graduated from high school. Oh, well. We all have our own unique giftings.

When my brother was in his senior year of college, he had to write and film his own movie. I was fortunate enough to become one of his esteemed actors. For my part in the movie, I had to walk an imaginary dog on an imaginary leash through the streets of the Upper West Side of New York City. I walked around Broadway and 116th Street, holding a ball, pretending I was walking a dog that wasn't visible on a leash that didn't exist. I must say, people all around me thought I was crazy. I guess that's what made it so much fun.

This set my brother and me on a course of talking about, reading about, and enjoying movies throughout our lives. I am grateful for this, because I no longer see just the rudimentary story that's in front of me. I can find intent and purpose, and that has made the whole movie experience much more enjoyable.

What I've found has confirmed what I'm saying about love. Movies rarely get made unless love is somehow connected to the message. Even the most horrible fright movies have at their core someone who has been hurt or wounded through love lost, or something that's connected to it but turns out to be the polar opposite of love: abuse, torment, or debasement. I personally don't like these kinds of movies, but they weren't invented out of a vacuum. As they say, hurt people hurt people.

The writer's quest to pen the great American novel is equivalent to the film maker's desire to produce the world's greatest love story. Just look at the response to *The Notebook*. I remember entering the theater wondering if this was going to be just another chick flick. Of course, being the father of three girls, I have seen almost every chick flick ever made.

As the movie progressed I realized who the characters were from the two stories that unfolded before me. In spite of what I knew was coming, I still found myself caught up in the emotion of a young couple's growing love and an older couple's ability, or inability, to communicate that deep love once again. When it ended I was ruined. I sat there with tears pouring down my face and didn't move. I couldn't move. The woman on the other side of my wife (who was also crying) looked over at me, smiled, and said, "It's good to see a man with a heart." My response was "You'd have to be dead to not respond to that."

Isn't that the point? None of us wants to walk around with a dead heart. We want to have full lives. Lives filled with all the benefits love can bring. Isn't that why we these movies are so popular? We are all trying to rediscover what it means to really love.

Our present culture is so caught up in technology that on the surface it appears that we are no longer really human. To the casual observer we must seem like drones, moving about like mindless creatures blindly led by a small electronic device. It tells us where to go, how to get there, and whom we're meeting. It can answer almost any question we have, and do it—if we so desire—with a woman's voice speaking in an English accent.

But inside, beyond the ability for most eyes to see, is a heart that beats with a desire for more. More than what we have, more than what we see, and more than what we've experienced. We want more.

All the music and movies of our culture tell us one thing. They all point to a basic human truth: we are moved, motivated, and empowered by love. Love is all around us—either presenting a mirror before us, helping us to gaze back at our own lives and see those areas where we need to be inspired, where we need to grow in love; or giving us a clear window to see through, like Dorothy, and realize that love already exists all around us. He who has eyes, let him see.

My Love Project

When you next watch a movie or hear a song, go beneath the action or the sound. Look and listen deeper and you will discover a heart wanting more, a heart wanting love. What do you perceive? Be a person who can see more than what's right in front of you.

2

WHERE'S THE LOVE?

With all this love, what's happened to the world around us? One minute we're listening to a beautiful new love song or looking at another movie with another happy ending, then *BAM*, we're thrust back into the real world. And the real world looks very little like the world that songs and movies help to create.

Whenever I look at the news (I try to limit my intake), I'm confronted with all that's wrong in the world around us: murders, rapes, abductions, bombings, terrorism, human trafficking. All this and more is splashed before our eyes twenty-four hours a day, seven days a week. We can take a movie or a sports break, maybe lose ourselves in a good book for a while. But sooner or later it's right there again, reminding us that somehow, somewhere, there has been a disconnect—a disconnect from God's original intent for us.

From the moment we're born, we find ourselves on a quest for life. In the beginning it's all about survival. Food…drink. More food…more drink. Sleep…food. Fill diaper, empty diaper…more food. Actually, that might describe most of our lives.

We certainly were created to need, but not just food and drink. Our hearts were created to experience closeness to those around us. For every creature this starts at birth.

Research has shown that a strong initial bond between a mother and her newborn child can help prevent certain illnesses as well as increase a child's learning ability. A study from Ohio State showed that rabbits that were held and embraced increased certain hormone levels, helping the rabbits to withstand heart disease. The same type of hormonal increase takes place in children who are held and embraced as newborns.[1]

A study from Nagasaki University in Japan showed that the vast majority of newborns were able to differentiate between the smell of their own mothers from that of other mothers. For many of the children, the smell of their mothers alone could calm them down when they were crying.[2]

In the same study, over 90 percent of new mothers were able to distinguish and identify the scents of their children from multiple other infants. It also found that a child's scent will often trigger something within the mother's brain that produces a heightened devotion during the first few months of motherhood.[3]

Francesca D'Amato, MD, of the CNR Institute of Neuroscience in Rome said, "The mother-child bond assures infant survival in terms of protection, nutrition, and care. It's fundamental to survival."[4]

> We were made to bond in order to become healthy. Bonding equals healthiness.

I have four grandkids, so I end up watching a lot of nature shows. I was a little nervous when a couple of my grandkids watched a fierce-looking pride of lions prepare to pounce upon a beautiful young gazelle. I asked them if I needed to change the channel. My five-year-old granddaughter looked at me and said, "No, Papa, don't change the channel. It's okay. That's how the lions get their food."

Wow! She understood the "circle of life." As we watched, we noticed that the cubs, though fed last, got their meal because Mama was watching out for them. She did all the work. She ran the gazelle down and made the kill. She fought to get her share as well as her cubs' share. After much "interaction with her lion family," she broke off pieces of meat and brought them to the cubs. She also let them come to the kill when it was safe for them to do so. Over time they would learn this process themselves, but at this stage of life, a way was made for them. Mama was still bonding even while training.

Even before we are old enough to walk and talk, we begin a process that is quite beautiful.

As I watch wildlife shows with my grandkids, they always *ooh* and *aah* whenever babies cuddle with their mothers. So does my wife. From baby bears to lion cubs to alligators, mothers and babies form a bond that transcends almost all other types of emotional connection.

That bond is not just a childhood thing. It stays with the individual, and over time it forms the foundation of what becomes that person's view, or more precisely, his or her frame of reference for what it means to be connected relationally. If that initial connection is strong and meaningful, that bond will create a stability that puts down roots of security.

If that initial bond is weak or becomes broken, it puts down roots of rejection, mistrust, and a propensity to live a life of heightened comparison and competition. That continues throughout the growing years. Not surprisingly, disconnected, insecure, and rejected young people grow up to be disconnected, insecure, and rejected older people. Not the most fun way to go through life.

Let's say you put six or seven billion people on the same planet and have most of them go through life with some form of heartache, pain, disappointment, and hopelessness.

In a word, *disconnected*. You now have a recipe not just for broken people, but for a broken planet. Into all this enters man's innermost desire; that is, to be loved and to love others.

Now, I'm not saying that if someone had a wonderful bonding experience with his (or her) mother, he will live a long and peaceable life. Neither am I saying that if someone has a negative bonding experience, or none at all, he will grow up to be disconnected and lean toward a self-centered existence.

What I am saying is that from birth on up, we need to be connected to that which brings us life. Love begets love. We tend to live out of what we've lived in. And that's not just true for infants. If a child gets connected to the wrong crowd, he will do that which is both modeled to him and forced upon him. We need to be connected to love. Authentic love. God's love.

In my college psychology class, the instructor asked, "Can people function without love and affection?" Some students said no right away. Others, trying to prove either their deep inner strength or their asininity, said that people are perfectly capable of living without love or affection. A few went on to say that they were raised without any close personal bonds and because of that they were able to navigate life without a need for relational support or encouragement from others. A sad state of affairs, indeed.

Even in the church, following through with others and remaining connected has become a real challenge. Really caring for those around us is not always easy, but it's always right.

I once sat down with someone who had recently had a number of disappointing interactions with other church members. I listened carefully, expecting some bitter pill to rise up, but this individual was honest and sincere. I asked her to write out what she had just said to me. Then I asked her if I could add that to my book. She hesitated, but eventually said yes. Here is what this person wrote:

> I am weary of hearing "I love you" from people who never take the time to practically express it. Their words fall to the ground in a meaningless heap. Their words over time have never been followed up with any type of tangible expression of love, and though freshly given each week, they remain empty.
>
> I am saddened by what we place value on with people and what we're supposed to excuse because "that's just the way I'm wired." People expect us to accept their poor communication skills because "that's just the way I am."
>
> There seems to be no accountability for rudeness, mishandling people's hearts, or using others to help meet our needs or accomplish our agendas.

People will admit their weakness in following up relationally, but only to deflect the responsibility of actually following through relationally. Words without the correct deeds that follow fail both themselves and others.

It seems that over time, we've become used to the sound of clanging cymbals, and after a while we just get tired and end up calling it music.

Wow! That's an honest heart. People are hungry for real, authentic relationships, and all too often our weekly church interactions set people up for relational expectations that never find fulfillment.

We need to be careful how we speak to each other. We often want others to think that we love them, but our language can often set them up for disappointment. I often want to say, "Put the mouth down and step away."

Love well and encourage others, but make sure whatever you say is honest and truthful. Don't speak false expectations to others. Remember, a human heart is a mixed bag. It's not just strong; it's also very fragile.

There's an old song that has the chorus repeating, "Love stinks" over and over. Do you think this was written by a heart that was enraptured with warmth and tenderness? Or a shut-down and recently wounded heart? These kinds of wounds make it into our music and movies because they've first made it into our lives. That leaves us wondering, "If I'm going to get hurt again, why bother? The safest thing for me to do is circle the wagons, take out my weapons, and learn to protect myself."

When one hurt and wounded person links up with another hurt and wounded person, the results can prove disastrous. It's no wonder so many relationships have so many bumps in the road.

You've probably heard the generalized statistic that about half of all American marriages end in divorce. More accurately, 41 percent of first marriages end in divorce, 60 percent of second marriages end in divorce, and 73 percent of third marriages end in divorce.[5] As the wounds increase, so does the divorce rate.

According to a study by the University of Denver, living together before getting married can increase the chance of getting divorced by as much as 40 percent.[6] This study seems to show that it's wiser to strengthen the ability to make a commitment by living separately until marriage than to experience cohabitation as a form of "practice marriage."

If you feel the need to "test" the relationship, you may already know in your heart of hearts that it's not meant to be. So what's love got to do with it? Well, it appears an awful lot.

One important note. If you see yourself in one of these

statistics, let me just say that you are not a statistic. We can, by the grace of God, create our own paths…new paths. His mercies are new every morning!

I realize that this chapter is not as fun to read as the previous chapter. (It wasn't as much fun to write, either.) That's because reality usually isn't as enjoyable as fantasy. Isn't that why we steal away to read a good book, see an afternoon matinee, or put on headphones and drown out the world around us? The problem is that while all these activities can enhance life, for far too many people, they become life.

Every day, about twenty-one thousand children die.[7] Yet this tragedy rarely makes headlines. We dismiss the horror that takes place in the world around us, either because there is not enough time to unfold all the tragedies or because we are too overwhelmed with our own. We are working hard just trying to pay our bills, get our kids to listen to us, or figure out what keeps triggering our constant headaches.

If we were to look at the world through the lens of "what's the next problem?" our lives would be consumed by watching one tragedy after another. Though we may have learned about slavery in our history books, most people have no idea that at this present time, more people are being held as slaves than ever before. Most of them are used in the sex trade or as common laborers. As of this writing, there are twenty-five to thirty million slaves in the world. India alone has over fourteen million people being held as slaves. The US has approximately sixty thousand slaves.[8] Though that number is much smaller than in many countries, that's sixty thousand more than there should be.

When I was a little boy, I saw commercials that boasted that before the year 2000, worldwide hunger would be a thing of the past. In spite of that lofty goal, *The Lancet* medical journal estimates that malnutrition contributes to the deaths of 3.1 million children under five annually.[9] Even huge concerts with headliner musicians haven't put a dent in the problem. All too often, corrupt governments take the lion's share of funds donated for the children's food to use for their own selfish purposes.

This bad news isn't cutting-edge information. But even those who aren't aware of the specific facts are aware of the pain and suffering across our planet.

Without hope, the world presents us with a pretty morbid picture of life here on earth. Where's the love?

How do we handle such extreme situations and still have what it takes to tackle our own personal struggles? I think we all have a place in our hearts for the downtrodden and the poor. Yet at the end of the month we find ourselves trying to make sure that our water bill is paid on time.

No one is immune from inconvenience and heartache. It is part of the human experience. Neither health, wealth, nor religious beliefs can shield us from life's perplexities and trials. Then how do we turn our attention from ongoing pain to living in joy? What makes one person see the half-full glass and another see it as half empty?

The answer is the same commodity that empowers newborns: connection. For a newborn, connection is everything. And solid, authentic connections are needed by all people through every age. The act of needing others is inherent within humanity. Children need parents and people need friends. Simply put, people need people. When we start to think we've grown out of our need for others, things begin to go downhill.

Why all the songs about love? Because people crave affection. Why all the movies with happy endings? Because people are hoping that maybe, just maybe, their lives will somehow have that same kind of positive resolution.

How does that happen? In movies, the gulf created as the crisis is usually bridged by some expression of love that proves itself once and for all…usually within the last ten minutes. The hero comes through by arriving at just the right time to save the one in need. What people often don't realize is that movies, books, music, alcohol, and myriad other fillers are not, and were never meant to be, our great connection.

A real Hero is waiting for us to discover Him and His true heart for us. People talk about God and His ways as being mysterious. Rich or famous people only seem mysterious until we get to know them. Over the years I have met many people who appeared impossible to get to know. To me, they were larger than life, and for one reason or another, they seemed out of my league. Then something happened, and we found ourselves in the same world as each other, living side-by-side or working together on a project, and I discovered they were not so mysterious once I understood and knew them.

God is also real, with a unique personality and a desire to be known. We all want to be known. Not just for what we do but for who we are. The same is true with God. We were created in His image. The desire to be known was first in His heart, then He passed it along to us. God is too often celebrated for what He's done—you know, creating the world from scratch, parting the Red Sea, making water pour forth from a rock, turning water into wine. Those are all great accomplishments, for sure. But His greatest desire is that we would know Him. *Really* know Him.

To experience life and love as God intended, we must be connected to the one who created the human heart.

We have owner's manuals for everything we buy. When we can no longer figure out how to fix something (my computer and my cell phone come to mind), we contact the manufacturer. The right connection makes it all work right.

If you need food, you go to a grocery store. If you need your car fixed, you go to a mechanic. But when life begins to spiral out of control, most people don't go to the Source of life; they find a distraction of some kind, whether it's self-medicating, turning to another person (often someone inappropriate) to meet their physical needs, or simply filling their lives with distractions. The problem is, these people remain disconnected from that which will bring resolution and harmony to their situation.

You and I were never meant to find answers within ourselves. We were created to find life in bonding, and nothing brings us more abundant life than when we bond with the Source of life. Nothing releases more love from within us than when we bond with the Source of love. God is the Source of life. And He doesn't just give love, He is love.

> We will search forever for answers if we do not include God in our questions.

Science often starts with the concept that God does not exist. Beginning their theories from that frame of reference, they will always come up short.

We do the same thing when we try to live life without a real and personal connection to the Giver of life. The Love Project started in heaven. God desired to create a people who would see His goodness and volunteer their lives and their love to Him. Some might suggest that by doing that God displayed arrogance and a need for power. Actually, the opposite is true. He is the best answer for every need and situation, and He knows that. He is not turning our hearts toward Him for His benefit, but for ours. He knows that all of life's answers are met with Him, the Author and the Finisher, the Beginning and the End.

It's only right then to look at how He feels about us and what He desires for us to know about Him.

When I was in school, the teacher always made sure our books were closed when it was time to take a test. We couldn't look at our neighbor's test paper, and we couldn't raise a hand and ask the teacher what the answer was. But God is not that kind of teacher. He has the ultimate Answer Book, and He loves it when we get up out of our chairs, come forward, and ask for answers.

So let's take a look at what His Book has to say about how He sees us and how deeply He loves us. This project of the heart is the ultimate open-book test.

My Love Project

A lamp won't shine unless it's plugged in. In the same way, we have no light and no life unless we are connected to the Source. If you don't know God, seek a connection with Him. If you do know God, pursue a deeper connection. He knows you perfectly; He's just waiting to be known. A sincere and simple prayer will open the door.

3

THE BOOK OF LOVE

E very major religion has at its core the teachings of Jesus Christ. It's hard to argue against a message that speaks of loving one another, especially when that message was put to the ultimate test when its leader lovingly and willingly laid down His life for those of His time and for all times to come.

God is not just the inventor of love, He is love personified in the form of Jesus. Let's look at what He feels, thinks, and wants us to know about love.

The apostle John, known for his tender heart and intimate friendship with Jesus, said, "In this is love, not that we loved God, but that He loved us and sent His Son as the atoning sacrifice for our sins" (1 John 4:10).

I love that. John is not trying to point a finger at us and say, "This is love: you need to love God more!" He is saying something that, if we really comprehend it, will change how we live. Love does not start with us; it originates in the heart of God. What a revolutionary statement!

Just a few verses before this, John made the quintessential statement as to the supreme nature of God. Yes, God is kind. He is tenderhearted and forgiving. We say that He loves, which is true. But it's more than that. He doesn't just love. According to John, God *is* love (1 John 4:8). He doesn't just "do love," He is love! That means that nothing comes to us from Him that is not connected to and motivated by love.

Why do so many run from God? That is one of life's greatest mysteries. If we only knew how He feels about us, we would run to Him instead of away from Him.

John goes on a few verses later to tell us where our love comes from. He wrote, "We love Him because He first loved us" (1 John 4:19). To most people that verse describes the chronology of love in our lives. First God loved me. And then, at some point, I recognized it, responded, and loved God back. That's true. And my prayer is that the world would know His love and truly respond in kind. But there is more to this verse than just a time line of how love is expressed.

This verse also gives us an invitation to unlock a secret as to how to grow in love. "We love because He loves us" could also be written, "We have the capacity to love to the extent that we know we are loved by Him." Our ability to love is connected to how deeply we know we are loved. Wow!

For so long I tried to love God and love people because I knew it was the right thing to do. Trying to do the right thing is not bad, but it has a short shelf life. Before long, loving others becomes harder to muster up from within yourself. But when I am enlightened by the revelation of how deeply God loves me, my capacity to love increases as the knowledge of His love for me increases. It's like those bar graphs from school. One bar—my ability to love—is always linked to and dependent upon the other bar—the knowledge of God's love for me. It's good to love, but it's *great* to know how to grow in love.

We humans fail miserably, and often. It's easy to love people when they are nice to you, give you gifts, and talk about you in flattering ways. We assume that God is like us, loving us when we're nice to Him, when we talk to others about Him, and when we go to church or give someone on the street corner some money.

That changes, though, when we feel we have messed up. We then go into "human God mode." We expect God to respond to us in our messed-up condition the same way we would if someone around us messed up. We equate our feelings of shame as being similar to the attitude God has for us at the time.

Fortunately for us, God does not change. There is not even a shadow of change with Him (James 1:17).

> Therefore, my ability to mess up does not change God's position of love. He is steadfast in who He is.

That's not a permission slip to continue in any wayward activity. There is always a price to pay for being foolish. All I'm saying is that my foolishness does not change His loving-kindness.

The apostle Paul, who wrote much about love, spoke to the strength of God's love for those who love Him. His letter to the Romans says, "I am persuaded that neither death nor life, nor angels nor principalities nor powers, nor things present nor things to come, nor height nor depth, nor any other created thing, shall be able to separate us from the love of God which is in Christ Jesus our Lord" (Romans 8:38–39).

What an amazing passage! Looking over that statement, it's hard to add to his list. What else is left? There is absolutely nothing that can move God away from His position. He is steadfast in His love for me.

Okay, He loves me, but how? The simple answer is *in every way possible.*

King David understood what God's heart was like. As Scripture describes him, he was a man after God's own heart (1 Samuel 13:14). I used to believe that "after God's own heart" meant that David pursued God's heart with a steeled determination. Kind of like a runner who is running a race with all his might, or someone who is running after someone who is faster than he is. If that were it, I would be more than a little discouraged. I can pursue God, but if it's a race against Him, I don't stand a chance.

One day at a wedding, while standing in the reception line, I heard an older woman say how much the groom took after his father. The groomsmen were his brothers, and this woman expressed amazement at how each son took after their father. A light went on when I realized that the term "after" was not to "run after" but to "take after." A very different meaning. When I got home, I checked the Scriptures, and sure enough, the original Hebrew translates that passage as "a man *of* God's heart."

So how was David able to view God's heart? For one thing, he saw God not as a God of wrath, but as a God of mercy. To David, God was a father. In Psalm 68:5 David writes of God as "a father of the fatherless, a defender of widows." Then he states, "God sets the solitary in families."

What a caring Father He is, for according to Psalm 10:14, He is "the helper of the fatherless," and in Psalm 146:9 He, as a Father, "watches over the strangers" and "relieves the fatherless and widow."

In Psalm 139 David gives us a clear picture of how God

thinks of us. Toward the end of one the most beautiful and poetic psalms ever written, David shares God's thoughts, and they are amazing. He says, "How precious are your thoughts to me, O God!" God's thoughts of us are precious. Its meaning is that His thoughts about us are beautiful.

> God thinks beautiful things about me?
> Yes, He does!

And not just one or two. Verse 18 says, "If I should count them they would be more in number than the sand." More precious thoughts than grains of sand in the world? Wow! That's a lot.

Let's break this down a bit more. A milk pail can hold over two billion grains of fine sand. And that's just one pail. Now imagine a truckload. Now imagine a beach. Brain freeze! It's time we realize that we are loved perfectly by the one who is perfect.

Though God is one God, the Bible gives Him many names and titles. Those who love and follow Jesus are called the bride of Christ. That would make Him a Bridegroom. Let's look at this heavenly picture of love.

Heaven is in preparation for a wedding ceremony called the "marriage of the Lamb." From Revelation 19:7–9, 21:2, and 21:9, it's clear that some kind of bride is being prepared for Jesus, the Lamb of God.

As a father, I have the joy and privilege of loving my children in a way that produces roots of security. If they are convinced that they are loved, not just for their positive actions but for who they are, those secure roots go down deep.

But my children are not intended to live with me forever. At some point in time, they will be captured by a different type of love. One that not just secures them as people but that lets them soar into who they're created to be—a love that continues to mature, multiplying that love to many more over time.

At their weddings, I walked my daughters down the aisle, hoping they felt secure in their father's love, giving them to another man, and to another kind of love that would allow them to grow into the women and mothers they longed to be.

Jesus, our Bridegroom, wants to lavish a specific kind of affection on us that is seen most purely in His role as our "life companion." (Note that the role we have as the bride of Christ is not a sensual or sexual connection to Jesus. Romancing the heart to unlock love is a beautiful thing, but seeing our role with Christ as something carnal is a big mistake.)

When I got married, the pastor who married us said to me, "Chris, everything that has been yours now belongs to both of you. That means your motorcycle is also now hers.

Even your guitar now belongs to the two of you." It was meant as a joke, but it struck a chord in me. The same thing is true for the great Bridegroom and His bride.

If I am Jesus' bride, I have His protection. If I see myself as His bride, I will understand that He wants to share all that He is and all that He has with me. I get His name and I get His never-ending love.

Yep, I think it's wise to see Jesus as the Bridegroom as well as my Lord.

To discuss the subject of love, we must understand that love is not just some fluffy feeling that rises up and overtakes our reason. Sometimes the most loving thing doesn't feel warm and fuzzy at all. Both the Old and the New Testament speak of love as being a caring discipline from a loving Father.

Proverbs 3:12 says, "Whom the Lord loves He corrects, just as a father the son in whom he delights." What a sweet way to express a challenging truth. In the New Testament the Word again expresses God's chastening love as being from a father. Hebrews 12:6 reads, "Whom the Lord loves He chastens." Love and chastening bundled together. It's a vital and necessary truth that we must embrace if we are to get the full counsel of God and understand how He loves us in a complete way. I don't want to miss out on something from God because I'm a little "put out."

Years ago, when my brother and I took our families to

Letchworth State Park in Upstate New York, I heard my brother scream out his son's name as his little boy was approaching a cliff. This was no subtle shout-out; it was a scream heard by all who were within a mile. This yell of love was not a soft and gentle expression of love, but a truthful shout to the heavens.

My nephew, knowing his father's voice, stopped immediately. A moment later he began to cry because his father had yelled at him. He didn't know that his dad's yell might have saved his life.

> The truth can hurt. But Jesus always delivers the truth in the package of grace.

John 1:14 says that Jesus came to earth "full of grace and truth." God speaks all of His corrective truth with grace and in love. This gives us the opportunity to mature and become all that God has designed for us to be. The apostle Paul told the Ephesian church that when we speak the truth in love, we will "grow up in all things into Him who is the head—Christ" and cause "growth of the body for the edifying of itself in love" (Ephesians 4:15–16).

I hesitate to use the expression "Love is like a..." because it can become such a corny exercise. But after looking inward at something I try to live out, I have to share one. Here goes.

Love is like a garden. We are called to water other people's gardens through genuine affection and encouragement, but we're never called to weed them. My philosophy is simple: weed your own garden and water other's. We can be assured that the Lord will correct those He loves.

From Genesis to Revelation, God's Word contains messages that can awaken our hearts to the life-changing love of God. He covers our sins, becomes our peace, whispers sweet words of affection, and prepares a place for us to join Him in eternity. From beginning to end, He wrote the book of love. Let's read it. It's full of life!

My Love Project

We can only love to the extent that we know we're loved. Do you believe God loves you? The Bible has been called God's love letter. To be a student of love is to be a student of God's Word—the book of love. Pick up your Bible, read Psalm 139, and explore God's affection for you.

4

<<<<<<<<<<<<<<<<<<<<<<<<<<<<<<<<<<<<<<<<<<<<<<<<<<<<<<<<<<<<<<

THE GREATEST OF THESE

One of the most common sections of Scripture read at weddings is from what has been called the Bible's love chapter: 1 Corinthians 13. Because these words are so often associated with weddings, I have noticed that this passage does not get its due outside of that ceremony. This chapter of the Bible should be front and center not only in our churches and our homes, but first and foremost in our hearts.

The chapter not only defines love, it also tells us what God is like. We can insert God's name whenever the word *love* is written. God is love, and this chapter describes the parallel truths of God's loving nature as well as His invitation for us to walk in that nature, being people who love well.

While my focus in this chapter will be on verses 4 through 8, it's important to hear God's introduction to the subject of love. He starts by saying that even if our ability to articulate truth is amazing, if we do so without love, we are nothing more than noise. He actually says we become a clanging cymbal. In other words, it hurts! Possessing marvelous gifts—such as the ability to prophesy, to understand all mysteries and all knowledge, or to demonstrate incredible faith—means nothing to Him unless we walk in love.

Whoa! That's a whole lot of spiritual activity that has no value unless it is worked out in love.

What are we looking at during this present church age? Do we have His heart to understand that, though our message may be filled with great truth and insight, without love it has little intrinsic value in the kingdom of God?

> Even if we give away all of our resources, from money to our very own bodies, it will profit us nothing if we live without love.

Now, that's an introduction!

So if I'm supposed to have love, how does God define that word? Let's take a look.

◇◇◇◇◇

Verse 4 says that love is patient and kind (NIV). Another translation says, "Love suffers long and is kind." I love this about God. I'm not so sure about me. Suffering is bad enough, but to do it for a long time and to be kind in the midst of it, that's asking a lot. But that's what love does. Love has the capacity to endure.

I am always amazed when I meet nice, friendly people and later on discover they are dealing with a situation that would have put me on the "victim's alert list." If I'd been in their situation, I would have let someone know about my plight. But not those who have learned how to suffer long and be kind. What a gift to have, and what a gift it is to those around them.

✕✕✕✕

Verse 4 continues, "Love does not envy." Imagine a world where your gain is my joy.

I've noticed a strange thing among humanity, both the churched and the unchurched. When someone is hurting and found to be in great need, people drop what they're doing to run and help. It is a glorious thing, and I always love to see it. But when something wonderful happens to those around us—a new job or raise, a new car or a new love—people rarely ring a bell and shout "Yahoo!" from the rooftops.

That's because most people desperately want those things for themselves. And envy, with its mighty talons, grips hard upon the heart, releasing pangs of jealousy and comparison that run deep. We often run to help others in their weakness so that we can feel strong and appear whole. But when someone around us is being blessed, sometimes envy kicks in. Envy is ugly. It can destroy even the closest of relationships.

Love, on the other hand, is free from comparison and can rejoice even when those around us are enjoying liberal blessings yet it appears that nothing is coming our way. I said *appears* because we often miss God's goodness when we have a preordained idea of how we should be blessed. When His blessings come to us another way, we don't see it as His love.

I heard a story a while back that made me both think and laugh. A group of people who were all going through personal hardships shared their stories with each other. As each one shared, he or she threw into the middle of the group an object that was symbolic to that situation. After hearing about all the heartache and pain that all the others were hearing, they each had a chance to pick up whichever object they desired, symbolizing that they were taking someone else's pain and hardship, believing it to be a lesser heartache than their own. To the surprise of everyone, each person chose his or her own burden. When asked why, they all had a similar answer. "I don't like what I'm going through, but at least I have grace for my situation. I can't imagine having to carry what so-and-so has to carry."

Don't envy others. You never know what's going on in their lives. And God has all the grace you need for your situation. Don't ask for another life. You may get more than you bargained for.

∞∞∞

This passage goes on to say that love "does not boast, it is not proud" (NIV). Now, if anyone could boast, it's God. I mean, really! When did you make a living creature out of dust? Ever create a star or set a moon in a perfect orbit? God has every right to boast. But He doesn't. Why? Because love is not boastful or proud. *He* is not boastful or proud.

A couple of years ago I saw a friend I hadn't seen in many years. We enjoyed a lunch with our wives, and I was excited to see him. When he asked how I was doing and what was happening in my life, I went off like a wild man, telling him this and that and everything else.

When my wife and I got back in the car to leave, she said, "What was that?"

"What do you mean?" I asked.

She went on, very lovingly, to tell me how I sounded. In a nutshell, I came across as boastful. I was embarrassed and sought the Lord on this. He confirmed my wife's evaluation.

If there is boasting to be done, boast about the goodness of God or His faithfulness in the lives of those around you.

Don't be proud of your accomplishments, but in the most sincere way, take pride in how you do them. That is, let your works be done with a spirit of excellence. If there's praise to be rendered, let it come from the mouths of others.

◇◇◇◇◇

Verse 5 says that love "does not dishonor others, it is not self-seeking" (NIV). I keep these two together because they are intimately intertwined. I believe that if most of us heard the first part, "Love does not dishonor others," we would heartily agree and move on. But the next section is where the rubber meets the road. "It is not self-seeking."

How often do we do something for the praise and gratitude we'll receive when the giving is done, rather than for the selfless or altruistic purpose of blessing others? Letting those around us receive well-deserved honor without doing anything to direct it to ourselves is a beautiful expression of love.

> Be proactive and find out a person's need, and anonymously invest in him or her to meet that need. That is God. That is love.

Charity events are good, in that at the end, some commendable person or organization is benefited. But something is lost when at the end of the night the list of donors, including the amounts of their donations, are listed for all to see. Therein lies their reward. There is a better reward that awaits those who learn how to honor others while not seeking their own fame or gain.

There are three things that Scripture encourages us to do in secret: fasting (Matthew 6:18), praying (Matthew 6:6), and giving (Matthew 6:4). Why is it that so often we gather large groups of people together and tell them to do these things, knowing that multitudes of other people know what we're doing?

"Hi, Bob. You fasting too? Are you doing the twenty-day or the whole forty-day fast? Oh, you're just doing a Daniel fast. I see. Oh, well."

"How's your early morning prayer time going, Sandy? Are you doing the sacrificial giving commitment as well?"

I realize that as communities we engage in biblical expressions of life together, but the overemphasis can sometimes be a bit much. It's always a good thing to check our motives for what should be normal spiritual lives.

Most people have mixed emotions about giving, praying, and fasting without anyone knowing. But that's what love does.

◇◇◇◇◇

Verse 5 says, "It (love) is not easily angered" (NIV). That should be emblazoned on the outside of every car door. And before you can enter your vehicle, you should have to repeat this verse. And put something in the lock mechanism that can tell whether you're being sincere.

Love does not anger easily. Why? Because people who anger easily are usually trying to get what they want immediately. When they don't get it, watch out.

I understand anger. We've all been angry. But a lifestyle of anger indicates someone who has set himself on his own throne, thinking everyone should know what he wants and have it available when he wants it.

Often anger is connected to expectations that have not been fully realized. I recently read a list of demands for some popular celebrities as to what they required in their dressing rooms. Here are some examples:

- a late-model car with temperature set at 72 degrees
- white and pink hydrangeas
- rose-scented candles burning when they arrive
- all the brown M&Ms removed from a big bowl of candy
- a three-seat couch, plain in color—any color, just no patterns.

And this is the mild stuff. I kept the more bizarre and demanding ones off the list.

Sadly, Christians often have similar unreasonable

demands. The more entitled we become as a society, the higher our expectations become. The higher those expectations, the greater our anger will be toward others when they're not fulfilled. I love Paul's words to the Romans: "Because of God's gracious gift to me I say to every one of you: Do not think of yourself more highly than you should" (Romans 12:3).

Love does not allow anger to rise quickly when we don't get what we think we deserve.

∞◇◇∞

The last part of verse 5 says love "keeps no record of wrongs" (NIV). Wow, that's a big one!

"But Chris, some of the best ammunition I have against the person I'm arguing with is based on their past mistakes. If I can't use that, I'd have little to argue about."

Bingo! When we walk in the ability to process what's in front of us right now, our disagreements will be short and to the point, accomplishing what they were intended to accomplish.

In Psalm 103:12 David exposed the heart of God when he wrote, "As far as the east is from the west, so far has He removed our transgressions from us." I'm no scientist, but if an object goes continually east and another object goes continually west, I'm pretty sure they will never meet. Because of God's heart of love, our sins are to be removed and forgotten.

Micah 7:19 says that God will "cast all our sins into the depth of the sea." Some have called it the "sea of forgetfulness." God never forgets. And yet, He chooses not to remember our forgiven sins. Choosing not to remember—that is love.

Take your hurts and disappointments that you've received from others and send them to the four winds. Let love have its way. We have a choice as to whether we will remember someone's wrongs toward us. Some people find it nearly impossible to let go of their hurts. But new hardships come our way almost every day. It's time to stop working so hard to continually remember the old ones.

◇◇◇◇◇

Verse 6 of 1 Corinthians 13 says that love "does not rejoice in iniquity, but rejoices in the truth" (NIV). I love the way *The Message* says it. It reads, "Love doesn't revel when others grovel, takes pleasure in the flowering of the truth."

> God never delights in the weakness and failings
> of man. He is always hoping for people to come to
> the knowledge of the truth.

That's what love does. It desires truth to be lived out within and then through people. When we fail or fall, love doesn't smile and boast in its own position of strength. It is not the voice of mocking or condemnation that revels when another grovels. Love reaches down and becomes the power to lift the fallen.

I once watched a TV preacher tear into the failure of one of his peers. He railed against him time and time again, even questioning his salvation. Before long, however, his own sin was exposed. Then he started frantically searching all around for forgiveness and acceptance.

Spiritual principles can work both ways. We freely receive, so we freely give. But sometimes, what we erroneously or imprudently give, we regrettably and invariantly receive back.

◇◇◇◇

Verse 7 begins the crescendo in this passage. These four simple truths, if taken to heart, could change the world. If we take them to heart, we can change our world.

Again speaking of love, this verse says that love "bears all things, believes all things, hopes all things, endures all things." How is that possible? To bear all, to always believe, to hope always, and to endure till the end? That sounds impossible.

And the next verse says, "Love never fails." What? Up until that point, this was good teaching. But this is an impossible task.

Ah, that's the point. With man it may be impossible, but with God everything is possible.

Remember, this chapter is not just a list of things we need to do better. It's a description of God's nature. He bears all things, He believes all things, He hopes in all things, and He endures till the end. He *never* fails. He never has and He never will.

The Love Project is not the addition of new and nearly impossible tasks. It's the realization of God's perfect and loving heart, and His desire to not just link arms but to link hearts. Like David, we can see, feel, and experience God's heart. And God's heart can't help but rub off on us and help us to transform our world.

Faith is powerful and hope can carry us, but the greatest gift of all is Him…love.

My Love Project

Media sources show us the best voice, the best actor, the best athlete. The greatest people manage to rise to the top, but they only stay there for a season. Love, however, will always be at the top of God's list of greats.

Which aspect of 1-Corinthians-13 love do you want most to grow in your life? Do something today that brings that quality to life for those around you.

5

LOVE STORIES

I n 1970, the movie event of the year was a film called *Love Story*. It ended up being the highest-grossing film of the year as well as being named one of the top ten romantic movies of all time. It was nominated for seven Academy Awards, winning one for Best Music, Original Score.

The movie starts out as a simple love story between two people. What made it immensely popular was the animated and jocular dialogue between the two leads as well as the story line. Jennifer, played by Ali MacGraw, was slowly dying—of what, no one knew. Roger Ebert, the well-known movie critic, said of the unknown disease, "The only symptom is that the patient grows more beautiful...until finally dying."[10]

This movie was put out there as the ultimate expression of romance. And yet, the key line of the film, which quickly made its way into popular culture, falls flat in terms of what

I consider love to be. After her young husband apologizes for an angry outburst, Jennifer sums up her understanding of love by saying sternly, "Love means never having to say you're sorry,"[11] which is the advertised slogan for the movie.

I don't know about anyone else, but during my first year of marriage, love meant *always* saying you're sorry. As of this writing, I've been married over thirty-six years, and I can truthfully say that maintaining real and authentic affection can sometimes be hard work. But in spite of the bumps along the way, I wouldn't want to change a thing. My wife is my better two-thirds, and like so many men, I married up.

In *Love Story*, the rich, handsome, arrogant young man finally finds love, only to have it snatched from his hands by a tragic, and eventually deadly, disease. If you've seen it before, you know it's coming, but you hope, just maybe, that this copy of the film will have a different ending. The book had sold millions of copies, so most moviegoers, like myself, already knew the ending before walking into the theater. In spite of that we all knew that the real story was found in their journey to find love. Finding love keeps bringing us back.

Another movie that I thoroughly enjoyed, based on a Broadway musical, came out during the late '60s. *Oliver* was based on the Charles Dickens book *Oliver Twist*. This movie has one of the most magnificent songs I've ever heard captured on film. It's called "Where Is Love?" It's an exquisite combination of hauntingly beautiful music and a deep heart-cry for authentic love: *Maybe, just maybe, something called love could actually be real.*

The world today is full of news. Most of the time we just get the bad news. I want to tell some stories where love wins.

> Love is real, and it's the greatest
> and strongest force on earth.

It changes people for the better. It gives people grace for the most impossible of tasks. And it gives hope to people that they too can live in love. So sit back and enjoy some real love stories that answer the question in the *Oliver* song.

This first story is of a young man who wasn't even looking for love. He was content in his bachelorhood, with no one on his horizon as a potential mate. He did not pursue love; love pursued him. I love it when love overtakes someone. It's fun to watch.

Rather than rewrite his story, I am leaving it as it came to me, in his words and from his perspective.

Throughout my journey, love has taken many definitions—most of them vague and few of them purely true. Indeed, the true definition of love is perhaps the very object of our "journey," for it is because of the Father's love that we exist in the first place.

Like too many of us, I grew up learning all the wrong ways to love. I saw my parents kiss once. I remember feeling an incredible warmth spread through me and I felt safe, happy, and at peace. I do not remember how old I was, nor do I remember that feeling again during my parents' marriage. I was somewhere around ten when my parents divorced, and it took me fifteen years to realize any psychological ramifications.

Counterfeits are only obvious when compared to the real thing.

I met my wife three months before I noticed her. For those three months I had consistent encounters with her and her child. Nearly every day I spoke to her. For years, even during this time, the Lord had been so gracious to protect me romantically (meaning I had very little interest in women and thought even less about marriage) that I fully anticipated living contently as a bachelor. If a girl happened to step into the picture, it was very easy, if not instinct, to remind myself how content I was with the Lord and that I had no desire to take on the responsibilities of being a boyfriend, husband, or especially a father, and on I would move.

One day I was throwing the Frisbee around with some friends when an incredibly attractive woman caught my eye. She was sitting a good way off, talking with someone. I asked the nearest buddy, "Who's that girl?" He looked at me like I had asked him in Portuguese.

"What?" I asked, slightly offended by his expression.

"Seriously, dude?" He proceeded to tell me it was the very girl I had known for three months.

In an instant, God opened my eyes to be able to see her.

I pursued her for three days, and on the third day I knew I was going to marry her. It did not matter that she had once been married. It did not matter that she had a child. All the reasons I had used in the past to convince myself not to pursue a relationship would not work.

Love was no longer conditional. The insecurities I'd harbored since childhood melted away. This woman loved me for who I was, and I found I was fully capable of loving someone unconditionally. I knew it was with this love that the Father had loved me, not the "love" I had grown up with.

His sense of irony is remarkable. He gracefully shielded me during my parents' split, and then brought me out of the victim side of divorce and placed me in a position to help heal a circumstance caused by divorce. Furthermore, since then, both of my parents' lives have been fully redeemed, and they live every day in love with Jesus.

Twenty-five years of broken, incomplete, and distorted definitions of love were immediately revealed as lies because God chose to reveal the truth in His perfect timing. And when God chooses to reveal some part of Himself (truth) to you, there is no choosing against it, there is no convincing yourself otherwise. It is written on the tablet of your heart and you are transformed.

My own journey is very similar to the story above as I met and got to know a young girl named Laura Rocissano. Though my last name is French, I am mostly Irish. My father was a mixture of French and Irish, and my mother's maiden name was Mary Katherine Murphy. You can't get much more Irish. I knew very few Italians growing up in the small town of Marion, New York.

After Laura and I met in 1977, we found ourselves in the same mix of friends, hanging out at the local coffee house or grabbing a pizza with the gang after some event. Laura was always kind and had an easy way about her. I told someone that someday I wanted to marry a girl like

Laura. I didn't know it then, but I was falling in love with the person, not the dream.

One day I was at a friend's house when in walked a few of our friends. I turned to my roommate Glenn and said, "Who is that girl with the dark hair?" He looked at me like I was from another planet.

"That's Laura."

"Laura who?" I asked.

"Laura Rocissano."

I couldn't believe it. She was beautiful. What had I missed up to that point? At that point I realized a false way of thinking within myself. I had believed that love would fully strike me all at once. Like in the movies. You always know who will get together in the end. It may take a while, but eventually it will happen. In life it's not always that way. Love snuck up on me. I fell in love with the person within and then became captured by her external beauty.

When we're young, we think we know what we want. But over time we grow and mature as people. And suddenly what we once saw as good becomes absolutely beautiful.

Love is not limited to young people searching for a spouse. Some of the greatest expressions of love occur between friends or family members. Even total strangers can show an unusual level of love toward someone in need. We refer to it as the kindness of strangers. What is actually happening is that someone is displaying genuine affection—love—with nothing expected in return. That's the purest kind of love.

We're told in Hebrews 10:24 to "spur one another on toward love and good deeds." That's my heart's desire with this book.

We are God's hands and feet. We have the opportunity to reveal His heart through our actions and through the attitude we carry during it. Often we put down "good deeds" as lower-level "good works." That is, we excuse ourselves from doing good because we associate that type of activity with trying to earn our way to a more spiritual place. That's nonsense.

As Paul says in Ephesians 2:10, we are "created in Christ Jesus to do good works which God prepared in advance for us to do." Before we were born, God had a plan for us to not just receive new life in Him through faith in His Son, but to take that life and lovingly display His heart through our good works to a world in need.

Our good works are not meant to be great spiritual achievements. Often they are an invitation to love through hiddenness.

The following stories are not what most people would call love stories. But love is not meant to be categorized into a specific expression. Love in its simplest form is the nature and heart of God. It's His desire and personality released upon the world.

I am blessed and convicted by this first story. So often we look for, even live for, convenience.

> Love, though, looks past convenience
> as if it doesn't even exist.

It's so easy to pull back from something that will require something of us. Love doesn't think that way. A loving heart is sometimes on the lookout for inconvenience.

As I left my meeting today in downtown Minneapolis I noticed a woman. She was huddled in a doorway trying to sleep. Tarnished copper pennies lay on the step below her stoop. They are of less use to her than to the people who threw them at her.

I've never done this before, but I couldn't help myself. I drove around the corner and bought her lunch, then came back with it. I touched her gently to see if she was awake, not wanting to scare her or endanger myself by getting into the space of a frightened, homeless stranger. I told her I had brought her lunch. "I'm cold," she said.

I realized, like really realized, she was lying on the concrete. Why have I never processed that before? I get all out of sorts if the air in my sleep number bed needs adjusting. A few degrees off the optimum room temperature affects the quality of my sleep dramatically as well. She sleeps *outside*. On the *ground*.

"Can I help you with your blankets? Try to make you warmer?" She nodded.

I kept touching her, not even realizing I was doing it—running my hand up and down her arm as she told me about her sleeping bag getting stolen. A tear ran down her face. Maybe it was the frustration of having the sleeping bag stolen, but I had to wonder. How long has it been since someone with no agenda has touched her? Imagine an existence without the humanity of touch.

"I'm not carrying a spare blanket, but I'll go look for a sweatshirt or jacket in my car."

"Do you have any socks?" I told her just the ones I was wearing, but I'd be happy to give them to her. "Oh, but you need your socks."

"No, I don't. It's okay. I'm going home." I gave her my socks, apologizing they weren't warmer and feeling the weight of those words—"I don't need them; I'm going home." Home. To a drawer full of socks. Right.

She asked for a few dollars so she could eat again later. I told her I didn't have much cash, which was why I'd gone to the store and bought her food—so I could use my debit card. Ouch, I just did it again. "So I could use my debit card." I told her I'd run back to my car and see what else I had for her.

I've been carrying a spare yoga mat—different practices, different rooms call for different thicknesses. This one's extra thick, dark brown. Perfect. I grabbed it.

"Would you like this? Would this help you sleep better?"

"Yes, oh, yes. Thank you."

"What's your name?" I needed to know. It was like the touch. I wanted her to feel like a person.

"I'm Cynthia."

"I'm Stephanie."

"It's nice to meet you, Stephanie. Thank you for your kindness."

I didn't know what to say. After a semi-uncomfortable pause, "Can I pray with you?"

"Man, I gotta get to a bathroom."

"Okay, I'll just pray for you by myself. Good-bye, Cynthia."

I'm grateful for the opportunity to love. I don't want people to think I'm sweet or kind.

And I don't want to be told that she is a drug addict or an alcoholic or whatever. I don't care.

She lives in a doorway. And how can I *not* care about that?[12]

I taught junior high school for seven years. Early adolescence is a difficult time in a child's life. They are no longer little kids but they are not yet adults. They live in humanity's "nowhere land." When a junior high school is combined with a high school, seventh- and eighth-grade students usually find themselves at the bottom of the food chain.

With my understanding of the hearts of kids at this age, the following true story brought tears in my eyes.

A young college student doing his practicum was assigned to a junior/senior high school in his city's suburbs. It didn't take him long to realize that class warfare was going on in that school.

A very kind and respectful young girl in eighth grade was constantly being teased behind her back. The young teacher tried to help, but he could only do so much.

At the other end of the spectrum was a senior boy who was handsome, athletic, and constantly surrounded by friends.

As the year came to a close, the school put on a talent show. When the teacher found out that the young eighth-grade girl had signed up to sing, he thought about stopping her, but he knew he couldn't. The show must go on. Still, he was dreading the event.

The evening of the show arrived, and student after student surprised their teachers and fellow students with their wonderful talents.

When it was time for the young girl to perform, she took the stage. But as the song began, she became flustered, lost her place, and sang slightly out of tune and with a wrong beat.

The kids in the audience whispered and laughed. The young teacher was devastated. But the young girl, with tears about to choke her, continued to sing over the growing noise.

Suddenly, the handsome senior started clapping to the beat, which helped her get her timing right. That enabled her to find her voice, and she finished strong.

When the song ended, the entire audience exploded in applause. The smile on the girl's face at the end of the song said it all.[13]

> Honor and respect are sometimes the greatest
> expressions of love we can give.

I'm sure that eighth-grade girl never forgot that twelfth-grader's kindness, and his example had a profound effect on all those around him.

This last story is from two people I know personally. I

see their love for each other on a regular basis. They are kind to each other and each prefers the other one on a regular basis. You'd think they just fell in love last week.

I knew Pete long before he met his wife. No one ever thought Pete would marry. But Sarah had something to say about that.[14]

I met Sarah during a time of life when I was very happy as a single man. I had considered myself a celibate for many years (two years actually living a monastic, hermit existence), and dating/marriage was still something with negative connotations to me due to the time and focus I believed it took away from my pursuit of the Lord. When I met Sarah, it had been fifteen years since I had been on a date.

Three years later, after gradually becoming good then best friends, my heart changed—completely. My thoughts on marriage and dating did not change very much, but I would do whatever I had to do to spend as much time with this girl as possible. Because much of my identity was wrapped up in being a celibate monk, the ramifications of changing my relationship with Sarah into a romantic one were drastic. However, it soon became clear to me, after my heart change, that this was not a choice I was able to make. The love that was exploding inside of me had to be shown. This girl, regardless of how she responded to me, needed to be shown the love I had for her.

My heart, though having experienced shadows of love as a younger man, seemed to double and triple in its capacity every moment I spent with Sarah, and then again every moment I was away from her.

Another thing happened that was desperately needed in my life—I began to experience a feeling of contentment. I believed I was only valuable to the degree that I did something monumental with my life. I had to be someone whom everyone knew to be worthwhile as a human being. My relationship with Sarah largely removed this from me.

I truly believe that my Sarah is the gem of the earth.

My goal became not "making something of myself," but loving this unbelievable gift that the Lord had given me in the most abandoned and un-self-protecting way I could. That was enough. In loving her, I was not concerned with how it made me look. She was the most amazing human being alive and she deserved to be loved in totality. How she reacted to that, or how foolish I looked or felt while showing that love, became irrelevant to me. I was a complete fool in love. This is something I never thought would happen between me and another person on earth.

Commitment was not something that I excelled in. I did not like the feeling of being tied to anything, whether it be a job, a ministry, a place, even people. I saw everything as temporary, and I longed for and thrived in change. In finding Sarah, I found the one thing outside of God Himself that was, in my opinion, the best thing that exists. I had no desire for change except to draw closer and closer to this woman and to love her increasingly more for the rest of my life. Why would I ever want to move on from that?

As a thirty-five-year-old celibate, my thoughts mostly revolved around myself and my pursuit of God. As Sarah and I approached oneness more and more fully, I began thinking in terms of "we" instead of only "me."

Shortly into our marriage, I became confused one day while washing in the shower because I could not find the scar on my lower back, only to realize later that I have never had one. Sarah had the scar, not me. The separateness between us was slowly but surely diminishing as I increasingly saw us as one entity and not merely two individuals. Love was making us one.

Love can surface in a person's life when he discovers an expression of love that he never knew existed.

> Love changes people. Give yourself time, and give yourself a chance to love well.

People need to see something more than the morbid stories that fill the channels of the nightly news. They need to know that there is hope to love. Too many families have too many stories of love gone wrong. Why not begin to write a new story of loving, of giving, and of expressing God's heart to those around you?

My Love Project

You may feel your story is not worthy of a book or a movie, but God sees it differently. Paul the apostle wrote in 2 Corinthians 3:2, "You are our epistle in our hearts, known and read by all men." Think about your own love stories and begin to write the book of your life with love. People are already reading it as they observe your life.

Every day is a new page. So turn the page on what went wrong yesterday and begin a new page today. His mercies are new for you today.

6

WHAT THE WORLD NEEDS NOW

At first glance, a man stranded at sea appears to have all the water he needs. In one respect he does. He has all the water he needs to float. But unless he has some pure water available, he will die of thirst right in the middle of an ocean full of water.

This is how I see our world. We are surrounded by all kinds of people. And yet many are dying of loneliness and starving due to a lack of loving relationships. How can that be? Unless you're living like a monk, it's pretty hard to live without being connected to other human beings who are on their own journeys of life.

The question for me is this: with more than six billion other people in the world, what keeps some from finding any sort of meaningful, satisfying, and loving relationship? Is it because someone else keeps them from it? Or is there something within us that for some reason does not allow love to enter the door of our hearts, let alone take up residence within us?

I have a dear friend who shared an apartment with me when we were single. We were in each other's weddings, and we and our wives are close friends to this day. When my wife, Laura, and I were new parents, we returned to the town where they lived.

We soon went to their house for dinner and a leisurely visit. My oldest daughter, Andrea, was a baby at the time, and when I asked my friend if he wanted to hold her, he pulled back and recoiled. I was totally surprised. He not only didn't want to hold her, his facial expression was a cross between fear and loathing.

I asked him to just take her for a second. He put his hands out, held her at arm's length like a sack of flour full of maggots, and quickly asked me to take her back. I did.

Our conversation quickly turned to the action I had just witnessed, and more important, the reason behind it.

He described some past experiences that had shaped his thoughts toward kids. Though his wife desired to have a few, he was fairly adamant that they would not be having children. They had discussed this before they were married, and it had not been a big issue. However, after their friends began having kids of their own, it became a problem.

> We often shape our present, and therefore our future, by the way our past has been shaped.

If we've had bad experiences with the baggage that comes with certain responsibilities (e.g., watching parents struggle and fail), we will try to shape our future by making sure we don't walk through certain doors (parenthood) so we don't pick up the baggage that's in that room (children).

But healing is available. And we can begin new seasons, even a new life. Just ask my friend who was afraid to hold my daughter. He finally got healed of his fear of children. He and his wife now have eight wonderful kids. Now, I call that a pretty good healing.

God is real, loving, and involved in our lives. And we are not our past, nor is our future a guaranteed repeat of our past. We have a choice. Life is not kismet. It has not already been determined by chance or detached destiny. But as Paul said in Romans 8:29, we are "predestined to be conformed to the image of His Son." That's as positive of a future as you can get.

This doesn't mean that God wants you to be someone or something completely different from who He made you to be. The world doesn't need Christian clones roaming around the earth all looking alike devoid of who He made us to be. The Father desires a lot of children who all walk in the fullness of who they are, with the fullness of Christ dwelling within them—each man and woman being fully alive, with the life of God fully alive in them.

What we're talking about is *identity*. Too often people try to answer the question of "What am I to do with my life?" before they have answered the question "Who am I?" To get there we must ask the right questions.

The first question humanity needs to answer is, "Is there a God?" This book is not a discourse or thesis on the existence of God. His quintessence, His very essence, is, to me, without question. Therefore, everything I write within these pages comes from the supposition that He is, always has been, and always will be.

When we answer the first question with an affirming yes, we then need to answer another of life's most important questions; that is, "What is God like and what does He think of me?" I lump these together as one question because how I see Him determines how I interrupt the way life comes to me.

In 2 Corinthians 3:17–18 Paul makes an almost *Braveheart* declaration when he says, "Where the Spirit of the Lord is, there is liberty." I liken it to *Braveheart* because when I hear that Scripture quoted in public, I often hear "yeses" and "amens" from those around me. It reminds me of the scene where William Wallace (played by Mel Gibson) rides back and forth in front of his Scottish countrymen, imploring them to go into battle for their own liberty. It crescendos when he ends with a thundering declaration that "they can't take away our freedom!" The men on the battlefield all yell and shout...along with the people in the theater. People love liberty. We desire freedom in our government; we crave it even more in our own lives.

The next word in these verses, though, is important. It's the little word *but*, which joins two thoughts together. The first thought is that the Spirit of God comes to bring us liberty. Wonderful! But the question is, liberty for (or from) what?

Verse 18 says, "But we all, with unveiled face, beholding as in a mirror the glory of the Lord, are being transformed into the same image from glory to glory, just as by the Spirit of the Lord." The liberty we receive is specifically for the purpose of unveiling our faces to see what God is really like. His Spirit wants nothing more than to reveal the glory (also translated as *beauty*) of God. Why?

> By seeing Him as He really is, we become transformed into the image that we behold.

The breakdown I have seen over the years is that often, the image people have of God is far removed from who He is and what He's like. That image we have of Him is vitally important. This Scripture says that as we behold Him, we are transformed into the same image. That's wonderful if we are seeing Him as He is. But if we have a warped view of God, I shudder at what we will be transformed into.

In over forty years of following Jesus, I have seen a dangerous pattern. The way people view the nature and personality of God often runs parallel to their own nature and personality. This has been the cause of untold wars over the centuries, and it's still pervasive today.

For example, when people see God as detached and uncaring, they carry in their own personality an uncaring detachment toward others. When people see God as leaning toward judgment as opposed to mercy, they become judgmental people who wouldn't know mercy if it slapped them in the face. Actually, if it were mercy, it would probably just give them a gentle kiss on the cheek.

If we see God as merciful and full of compassion, we begin to take on those characteristics ourselves. We become what we behold! What an amazing truth. That's why verse 17 makes us want to shout liberty from the rooftops. If I allow the Spirit of God to continue to pull back the veil, I will see more of Him, and therefore, I will become more like Him. Now, that's freedom!

Another aspect of beholding Him is related to His main identity. We all see God in a certain way, and we identify with what we see. He is many things, all of them glorious. But we all tend to lean toward one or two aspects of His position. This also consigns us to become what we behold.

This goes to the core of our identity in Christ. If we see His core role as a king, we become first and foremost subjects. If we see Him first as a judge, we assign ourselves as judged ones, always seeing our sin as opposed to His beauty.

If we see Him as our Master, we will see ourselves more as servants than as friends. Jesus said, "No longer do I call you servants…but I have called you friends" (John 15:15). If we see God as the general of heaven's armies, we will see ourselves as soldiers.

Now, are we His soldiers? Yes! Are we His servants? Yes! But my core identity is neither of those. I am a son! When I see myself as his beloved child, I see Him as my Father. When Jesus left the glory of heaven and came to earth as a man, He had two main objectives. The first is found in 1 John 3:16: "By this we know love, because He laid down His life for us." He came to give His life as a ransom so that we may be raised up with Him.

Jesus' other main desire was to showcase His Father as compassionate and merciful. Up until that time the main religious leaders had presented a harsh and judgmental God. When Jesus arrived, He immediately began to speak about this glorious Father He had known forever. Half of Matthew 5–7, known as the Beatitudes, is filled with references to the

Father rewarding His own, answering prayer, and making sure His children have all the provisions they need.

The entire chapter of Luke 15 records Jesus telling a story about a father who loves both of his children deeply, yet neither of them has the eyes to see what a wonderful father they have. Not until the younger son returns home and is met with a running, kissing, and restoring father does he begin to fully understand what a great man his father is.

Jesus could have devoted His life here on earth to unfolding any aspect of God's character, but he burned with passion to reveal Him as Father. Jesus wanted to model His Father's true makeup, inclinations, and temperament. Jesus said that He did nothing of His own, but only did what He saw the Father doing. He wanted to bring a shift to the falsehoods that the spiritual leaders of the day both taught and modeled. The scribes and Pharisees talked about a God who was distant and angry. Jesus, having lived eternally with His Father, knows Him like no other. He came to tell us, "My Father is nothing like those religious leaders. He is good, He is kind, He is forgiving. And by the way, He really likes kids."

When we see God as Father, we see ourselves as children.

To many, *father* is a four-letter word. It brings up a history of pain and bad memories. This is what God wants to heal. Jesus came to showcase a Father who is not like men. His Father can replace our pain with heaven's affection. He can turn our memories into scars, because when wounds are healed, the scars that remain become the toughest part of us.

This invitation goes out to those who would rather be soldiers than sons, or would prefer to work as servants rather than rest as friends. To the hardworking disciple, I ask, "Don't people who love their jobs work better and longer than those who feel obligated to work?" So it is in the kingdom of God.

Lovers always work better than servants.

I do a much better job on my own lawn than someone I hire when I'm on vacation. I, out of love, notice the little things. Workers have a job to do and usually look forward to getting the work done and leaving. I, on the other hand, look forward to seeing my lawn become beautiful piece by piece. Then I sit back and gaze at my work, enjoying its beauty, thankful that I have a lawn to mow and a place to call my own.

To love and be loved. That is each person's heart cry. Then why do so many people, believers included, feel lonely and isolated? It's not for lack of love, which is available to them. He dwells within all believers, and He is love, so His love dwells within us.

Saying it as fact is one thing, but living it out so that it makes a tangible difference in our lives is quite another thing. I was recently with some people, and I noticed one person who could not receive a compliment or praise from anyone. I tried to encourage this individual about something he had done. He nodded politely, but I could tell he did not believe or receive my words of encouragement.

This is in no way an isolated situation. Over the years I have witnessed scores of people who, for some reason, cannot take in the sincere love that surrounds them. Hurt and past disappointments can create within people the need to take every precaution to try to protect themselves from further hurt and disappointment. That is understandable. But I have seen the miracle of God's affection go deep within the human heart and heal even the most painful wounds.

> God is a loving Father, filled with the desire and the power to heal and restore every human heart.

He created you to lavish His love on you, and He wants to use other people to extend His loving heart to you. Let Him love you.

I try to make it a point in my life and ministry to highlight people not just for what they do but for who they are—not in some impersonal or isolated way, but in public settings where they can hear how people see them and feel about them. Time and time again, when people who could not receive a simple one-on-one compliment hear words of love and accolades of appreciation from their friends, they tear up, some crying almost uncontrollably. Sometimes it takes an avalanche of praise and approval to break apart someone's shield of defense. But when you see them in tears, embracing everyone around them, it's always worth the effort.

These people often tell me later that they were embarrassed and that they'll get me later. But when I say, "Honestly, how was it?" they always say, "Wonderful…and thank you so much for doing that." We all want to hear words that build us up and secure us in the love of others. The amazing thing is that when we hear those words first from our heavenly Father, we can accept them more easily from others.

Growing up in Upstate New York, I had a good handle on living within the seasons. Unlike in some areas of the world, there were four distinct seasons. Winter lasts a little longer there than in some places, but spring always comes and summer is always appreciated. We believers also have seasons, even with our relationships.

We may be close to someone while our kids are growing up. But when they become adults, that relationship changes. People change, and their life priorities change. So don't try to hold people, or the relationships you have with them, to a certain standard. They may have come to the end of a season, not just with you but with many. Release people to live and love where and with whom they are called to in the upcoming season. We don't own anyone, even our kids. We need to learn how to love people as the seasons change. We want that for ourselves. So let others receive that same form of honor and respect from us.

Learning to live as a conduit of love is important.

The Dead Sea in the Middle East has one major inlet—the Jordan River—but no outlet stream. Whatever enters the sea stays in the sea. Seas were not meant to contain all that enters. To be healthy, a sea needs an outlet so that all nutrients can be passed along, creating a flow that sustains life.

We must see with unveiled faces the glory and beauty of God, and in turn, freely give what we've freely received. Only then will we become sustainers and givers of His life and love.

It's not that people's eyes have been blinded to know *who* to love. All too often, people's hearts have been dimmed in knowing *how* to love. It's time for a new season. It's time to be loved and to love well.

My Love Project

We become what we behold, and how you view God determines how you live your life. So reflect now on how you see God. Pray for revelation of His heart for you. Remember Psalm 139:17–18. His thoughts to us are precious and good, and they number more than the grains of sand. That's a lot of thoughts and that's a lot of love. Immerse yourself in that truth today.

7

CHEMICAL ROMANCE
(THE SCIENCE OF LOVE)

While in high school, I joined many around me in denouncing science. Whether it was earth science, chemistry, or physics, we all asked, "How will I ever use it in my daily life?" Little did I know that not only would I have to apply science throughout my life, my life itself would actually become one huge scientific experiment: Start with compound A, add compound B, step back and watch what happens.

Relationship analysis uses similar terminology to science. When people have the ability to attract others to themselves, we say they have a certain degree of *magnetism*. When two people connect well, we say they have *chemistry*. If a couple's closeness increases, we say things are *heating up*. When a couple breaks up, we refer to their emotions in biological terms, such as *heartache* or someone becoming *heartbroken*. We talk of a relationship becoming *poisoned* or someone being used as a *guinea pig*.

Science can also be a mirror through which we view our lives. We see the tangible results of our actions—actions that always produce some type of reaction. Newton's Third Law of Motion states, "For every action there is an equal and opposite reaction." Second Corinthians 9:6 describes this law in biblical language. It says, "He who sows sparingly will also reap sparingly, and he who sows bountifully will also reap bountifully." The law of sowing and reaping is a law of science that God initiated. Therefore, it's wise to look at the areas of our lives that get our time, energy, and resources. To that which we sow, from that we will reap.

Our world all too often sows out of pain, and because of that, ends up receiving pain in return. What would happen if we sowed love, forgiveness, and kindness? What would be reaped, not just to those who receive those acts, but to those who originate the sowing?

The purpose of this book is to inspire and help you to grow in love.

> As you mature in love, you will become a person who gives love. That's how love works.

What happens within us as we grow in love and give that love away—not just spiritually, but also physiologically? Galatians 6:7 says, "Do not be deceived, God is not mocked; for whatever a man sows, that he will also reap." Our actions have consequences. Positive and negative.

Our bodies are amazing creations. The Miracle Maker designed us to function in the miraculous way we do. Then we grow in our own understanding of how to be responsible with the life we've been given.

Our bodies are constantly using energy, both positive and negative. One negative consequence of how life affects our bodies is increased stress.

According to the American Psychological Association, 43 percent of all adults suffer adverse effects from stress, and 75 to 90 percent of all doctor visits are for ailments and complaints that are stress related. Stress is often behind such problems as asthma, arthritis, headaches, high blood pressure, diabetes, and even major heart problems.[15]

In 2010, the Occupational Safety and Health Administration recorded that stress costs businesses in America more than $300 billion annually. Their research also showed that people in stressful relationships are at a much greater risk of developing depression and even weakened immune systems.[16]

From stress to poor eating, or drinking too much, or smoking, we are inundated with sowing and reaping examples. But what happens to our bodies when we sow to the Spirit; that is, when we sow positive, godly, and biblical virtues?

Are there positive results when we sow love, forgiveness, and kindness? Is there a link between actions of affection and our physical being? Though there are countless spiritual advantages that come to us as we sow to the Spirit, I want to look at a few physiological rewards.

Caroline Leaf, a cognitive neuroscientist with a PhD in Communication Pathology, wrote in a September 29, 2011, post from "The Science of Love":

> Being in love creates a positive chemical reaction that causes you to be physically healthier. A lack of love and affirmation can literally make you feel sick. Researchers are even finding that intense passionate feelings of love can provide amazingly effective pain relief. It turns out that the areas of your brain activated by intense love are the same areas that drugs use to reduce pain.[17]

Imagine if we could harness the power of love. Love is an untapped power, waiting for us to recognize its potential to change others and ourselves. Living loved is a prescription for better health.

Okay, I'm not a doctor, but I would like to give you a simple prescription. Here, I'll write it out:

Take two truths concerning God's love for you. Wash them down with a dose of affirmation from a loved one, and then give that love away to someone in need. You will get more love in return, causing your brain to send healing messages to every part of your body. You will soon feel much better. Call me in the morning.

By the way, there's no charge for this prescription. And since God's love is freely given, make sure your love is freely given to others as well.

Part of my prescription is connected to other people. Love is not meant to be lived out in a vacuum. "God so loved the world that He gave…" (John 3:16). He created the human race so that love could be expressed in innumerable ways, each individual mirroring His love, for "everyone who loves is born of God" (1 John 4:8). Every form of love is born from God.

> We need each other to fully express what love is and what love looks like.

Even without being physically present with a person, we can think healthy thoughts and create a loving connection that has real and tangible physiological affects within our bodies.

Conversely, we can also create negative reactions within

ourselves through toxic thoughts and feelings, such as unforgiveness, envy, bitterness, and jealousy. Each of these is a simple pill that, when ingested, has insidious side effects that work to extract the very life from the host.

People who isolate themselves are not doing themselves any favors. I understand we all need time alone now and then.

> Even Jesus took time away from the daily grind,
> but His purpose was not to become a recluse.
> His breaks from normal activities were to
> spend quality time with His Father.

He did this to strengthen Himself for loving and giving life to others. He said, "I have come that they (Jesus is referring to us here) may have life, and that they (again, us) may have it more abundantly" (John 10:10).

What happens to us when we are connected to others? Did you know that even the simple act of writing a love letter can actually reduce your cholesterol?[18] Writing letters slows down our emotional energy, allowing us to think more clearly, gaining better understanding and compassion, giving us greater clarity to say what we really want to say. Yes, change your diet and get some exercise, but include writing some love letters to lower your cholesterol.

Hugs are more than just a cute physical expression.

Frequent hugging between people who love each other actually lowers blood pressure, especially in women. Hugs are also linked to higher oxytocin in both men and women. Oxytocin is a hormone that makes us feel good. It lowers levels of stress hormones in the body, which reduces blood pressure, increases our tolerance for pain, and can speed up the body's healing process.[19]

According to a study from Stanford University School of Medicine, loving relationships activate neural receptors in the brain, releasing pain-soothing hormones that produce results similar to high-level painkillers. Because it's naturally produced, you get to feel better without the addiction that often results from synthetic painkillers.[20]

The Beatles broke through in the United States with a song called "I Want to Hold Your Hand." Its combination of driving sound, backbeat, and tight harmonies—mixed with the idea of a simple action, holding hands—caught the ears (and subsequently the wallets) of young Americans. It turns out that the Beatles were onto something. The uncomplicated and casual act of holding hands, particularly between people who have affection for each other (as opposed to two strangers, which brings its own set of potential problems) can create calmness and reduce stress.[21]

The present-day disconnect is more clearly seen in some present-day statistics. According to a March 2014 Pew Research Center study, millennials (those who reached adulthood about the year 2000) have been keeping their distance from marriage. Only 26 percent of this generation is currently married. When older generations were the age that millennials are now, significantly more were married—36 percent of Generation X, 48 percent of baby boomers, and 65 percent of the Silent Generation (those born during the Great Depression and World War II).[22]

The pursuit of loving relationships is happening later in young people's lives today. Presently, the focus of most young people is less about relationships and more about financial security. This same Pew study reported that almost 70 percent of millennials say they would like to marry but lack what they consider to be a necessary prerequisite: a solid economic foundation.

This speaks, not to a lack of love, but to a societal shift in love as a priority. For generations, the goal of finding love and sharing the ups and downs of life with another human being was of major importance. It is still important. But if the pursuit of love takes a backseat to economic stability, sooner or later the focus will shift from relationships to enterprise. When that happens, what's in front of us becomes more important than *who* is in front of us.

So where are we headed as a society? Will civilizations in future years talk about our time as the era when love was a popular subject to write about and sing about but not one to live for? Are all of our songs and movies there to make up for what we lack in reality within our communities?

I don't believe that's where we're headed. I have faith, not in the goodness of man but in the goodness of God. God is a better leader than we are followers, and He is leading us to Himself—love personified. He invites us to make love our top priority—loving God and loving our neighbors. God's love in us will fill us, heal us, and inspire us toward greater expressions of love toward those around us.

My Love Project

Try some sowing-reaping experimenting on your own. Encourage someone today and enjoy the encouragement you receive in return. See how giving people affectionate and encouraging comments releases the same type of communication to you.

LOVE THE ONE
YOU'RE MARRIED TO

When I was in middle school, I went through a huge growth spurt, and I once had to wear one of my sister's white shirts. She is seven years older than I, but with a tie hanging down the shirt I thought I would get away with it. Unfortunately, a girl in my class noticed that the buttons on my shirt were backward. Suffice it to say, that was a very embarrassing day for me.

The many differences between men and women can all seem backward. As little kids we realize boys are different from girls, and we're cool with that most of the time. As time passes we find ourselves in totally different worlds. After some years and trials, we may even have an epiphany that we have not reached a mature enough age or a deep enough understanding to appreciate the other's world. It's right about this time that many people get married.

Oh, we think we get it. We stand up before family and friends, telling the world that we will love and cherish our new spouse and that whatever tries to come between us had better watch out. I love watching people fall in love, and I love the weddings and honeymoons that follow. I have performed many weddings over the years, and seeing that fresh expression of love never grows old.

So why do half of American marriages end in divorce? If we were in a card game, and it came down to a 50/50 chance to lose our car or our home, the vast majority of us would stand up, throw down the cards, quit the game, and walk away. And yet, every year, more than two million weddings are performed across the US.

> Hope motivates us to do things
> we never thought possible.

Hope is an anchor that secures us in a storm and allows us to see the possible and dream the impossible. I love hope. But regrettably, people all too often marry on the wings of hope, without knowing that the realities of life—living together in peace, paying bills, raising kids, and feeling fulfilled as a person—can rock even the most secured and anchored boat. Life quickly teaches you what you don't learn by the time you're married about serving and giving your life away. Those who learn those lessons are wise. Those who don't may find themselves as a statistic. No one gets married thinking that he or she will become a statistic.

I married Laura Rocissano because I loved her, but I also knew her. She was beautiful inside and out (she still is), and I could not see myself spending my life without her. People often say, "I can see myself being married to so-and-so." During my dating years, there were many people I could see myself living with, but there was only one person I couldn't live without. That's a big difference.

As I stand before young couples, preparing to join them in marriage, I often have to keep my mouth shut. They've already been through some type of marriage counseling and believe they are ready to tackle this thing called marriage, and I don't want to say anything that would crush that beautiful thing called hope. But there's a high divorce rate in the United States for a reason.

In the apostle Paul's letter to the Ephesians, he tackled the subject of marriage head on. In chapter 5 he gives some words of advice for both husbands and wives. Some of what Paul says is controversial, especially what he says about women *submitting*. "Wives, submit yourselves to your husbands, as to the Lord." Wow! In our day and age, that's putting it out there.

What is Paul really saying? Well, I'll tell you what he is not saying. Paul is not using the word *submit* in a way that carries with it or implies any type of ownership. Too often I have heard men talk about their "woman" as if their wives were some kind of animal or object they owned. I've even heard the analogy of submission, as used in this verse, being akin to putting a bridle on a horse. This kind of thinking is absolutely disgusting.

Those who see this verse as justifying any form of domination of men over women are either misled or deceived. And any man who misuses his role as a husband for his own gain is a fool.

So how do we look at this verse in the context of today? Actually, the question should be, *How do we look at our culture in relation to this verse?*

Submission, in its purest form, is beautiful. It is an expression of wisdom and maturity. Submission is not a female thing. It's a human thing. I submit myself all the time to things around me. I stop at stop signs. I stay within the speed limit (most of the time). In school I submitted my work to the teacher, and at work I submitted myself to what was required. I submit to God, and I'm the better for it.

The meaning of *to submit* is "to yield." Isn't that what we're all called to do? In a healthy relationship, the one doing the yielding will receive the greater reward. Wisdom says that if two are to walk as one, they need to think as one and move as one. Yielding to each other is just a wise thing to do. The Bible instructs us to submit to one another in the fear of God (Ephesians 5:21).

But if a man has to use the word *submit* to his wife, something is wrong with his part of the relationship. His role is to love her as Christ loved the church. A church that knows it is loved by Jesus will easily partner with whatever He is saying. Why? Because of the trust factor. I trust that God is good because He has always been good. That's His nature. If a woman can trust her husband to be good and to put her above his other loves, she can easily trust him. Yielding to that man is easy because she sees that he holds her heart well and considers her as his equal, his partner, and that his decisions are not made out of selfishness but for their betterment as a couple.

How does a man love his wife as Christ loves the church? How can a weak human being even begin to compare with Jesus when it comes to love? We can't. That's why Ephesians 5 begins, "Be imitators of God as dear children. And walk in love as Christ also has loved us and gave Himself for us."

Jesus heard and saw the Father, and then did what He saw and heard the Father do. He was the perfect imitation of the Father on earth. As any good actor or comedian will tell you, the more you study someone's attitudes, actions, and heart motivations, the greater chance you will have of imitating that person.

I love great impressionists. They're my favorite type of entertainer. When they get the voice, attitudes, and inflections down, it feels like you're looking at the real thing. That's what we're invited into as men.

> The more we know of God's nature, thoughts, and heart desires, the greater chance we have of modeling that same heavenly personality in our lives and in our homes.

What woman wouldn't want to say yes to a man who prefers her wishes over his own? There's a reason young girls like to pretend they're princesses. They want to feel special and beautiful, and they're hoping that when the dragon comes their way with a fire that's out to destroy them, a prince will come riding in on a white horse and rescue them. When I put my granddaughters to bed, that's the story they want to hear almost every time.

If a man really understands that, he can become a hero in his own home. His wife and kids will be rooted and grounded in his love, and they will trust him with their very lives. We have the chance, men, to be princes. Oh, we'll come crashing down every now and then. That's just life. But if we're humble, and admit our failings, we will find ourselves being lifted onto a great steed, strengthened, equipped, and prepared for the next battle that awaits.

I know that many people have had difficult marriages, and this simple chapter is not the end-all solution for love and marriage. I was born at night, but not last night.

I was raised by a single mom after she spent years trying to make her marriage work. I have great compassion for people who find themselves at the marriage crossroads of life. I don't believe that a simple "Oh, go ahead and move on with the rest of your life" or the equally simple "Don't you dare separate or divorce" is effective. But if you're in that valley of decision, please ask yourself if you have exhausted every option for reconciliation before you "move on." There are biblical reasons for separation and divorce, but all too often the biblical road is bypassed for the sake of convenience. When children are involved, it is especially important to walk in as much light and godly support as possible. Ask God what to do, and more important, ask Him how to love. Our best response to any situation is always love.

My mom was my hero. I know how hard things were for her, not just emotionally but physically and financially as well. Being a single parent is not an easy road. The breakup of a home is never a pretty thing. Long-time friends taking sides and pulling away adds more pain to an already horrible situation.

And sadly, the church tends to shoot its wounded. Love may take some unique forms at times, but we are not called to tear Jesus' bride apart. We are to be a healing balm in the midst of heartache and pain.

If someone you know has come to the point of divorce, you may need to give this person more space if your friendship with the former spouse brings him or her pain. I've had to do that. But I did it with clear communication and the understanding that I was not taking sides. I understood the person's heart and the need to avoid further pain whenever this person saw my face and thought about what it represented. The goal is to give people room to heal, not to pull away your love and support. When your friend is aware of this, he or she can bring you back into a living and authentic relationship on his or her terms.

It's hard for me to write about separation when the focus of this book is to learn how to love with passion and intentionality. But that's the reality of love. It is most meaningful during life's most difficult times. It's easy to love someone when all is going well. What's not to love? When his boss just gave him a raise, or she has been affirmed in her giftings and made to feel accepted, it's easy to "let the love flow."

But what happens when your job goes away and the bills are due? Suddenly you are confronted with choices like which phone plan you should have or how "used" a vehicle should you get when your old car breaks down. When difficulties, misunderstandings, and ongoing tensions arise, God's true heart of love comes shining through.

Disney characters often fall in love at first sight. And they are awakened with love's true kiss.

> In real life, it's not a kiss or a look but the selfless giving of one's time, energy, and resources that show what love truly looks like.

Have you noticed that women look forward to the wedding day and men look forward to the wedding night? I've never heard anyone say, "I can't wait till we're back from our honeymoon and we go back to work and start to deal with life as a couple."

Why is that? Because most of us tend to view the future like a Disney movie. We will be prosperous. Our children will never fight or disobey their parents or teachers. We will never argue or even disagree about important things, because we really love each other. We will never be like "them."

It doesn't take long to figure out that you are "them." It's not the circumstances that come to you or even come against you. It's your response to those circumstances.

Love took Jesus to the cross. John 15:13 says, "Greater love has no one than this, than to lay down one's life for his friends." That is the essence of love. I believe that true love's kiss (a kiss from God) is a friend or spouse who continually lays down his or her life, preferring others on a regular basis.

A popular song in the '70s encouraged people to "love the one you're with." In one way that's a good thing. You should love those in your sphere of influence and those you're closest to. But that song isn't really about love. It's about saying yes to an immediate need, using someone right in front of you and temporarily forgetting about the one to whom you made a lifelong commitment.

If you're really going to love the people you're with, let them see Jesus in your speech, your demeanor, and your actions. But when it comes to the one you said "I do" to, give her or him your best. Save your heart and yourself for that one.

I want to encourage married people to have the humility to realize that you don't know it all. You are not weak if you ask for help. You are not wrong if you get counseling to help with areas of blindness. There is wisdom in the counsel of others. There are wise men and women who have gone before us. Don't feel that you need to carry it all on your own.

The greatest singers in the world, the greatest golfers in the world, the greatest musicians in the world, all have instructors and coaches—not just to get them to a place of excellence, but to help keep them there. Surround yourself with wise friends. Stay close to those who model affection in their lives and in their marriages. Be humble, and most of all, let yourself be loved by God so that you can love your spouse well.

Married people aren't called to love for a night or for a two-week honeymoon. Real love—selfless love—is found when the honeymoon ends. If a couple learns how to love God's way, the honeymoon never really ends.

My Love Project

Don't let our culture define you or your marriage. Be proactive with your affection, especially with your spouse. Take a moment today to tell your spouse *why* you love him or her. Then find one practical way to follow up your words with a meaningful action that expresses that love. Repeat daily. This will build strength within your partner that will spill over into every area of your life together.

9

TURN THE HEARTS, TEACH YOUR CHILDREN

I n my book *The Wild Love of God*, I describe growing up with a father who had been a POW during World War II. His release when the war finally ended brought him freedom, but the prison he had been in didn't end when the doors were finally opened. A new prison enveloped him, and upon his return there was still much pain within.

As the youngest of three, I ended up receiving the greatest amount of his anger and its manifested violence. My dad was a good man trapped in a cycle of abuse received and abuse given. From my vantage point, I didn't have years of perspective and a history of him before the war, which could have produced compassion and understanding. I only knew him as an angry man who brought fear to my heart and pain to my body.

Shortly after my salvation experience, I stumbled upon Malachi 4, which prophesied of a day when the hearts of children will turn to their parents and the hearts of parents to their children. These words are from the last sentence of the last chapter of the last book of the Old Testament. It is clear what intentions burned in the heart of God. He wanted to turn hearts. He is looking for hardened hearts to be softened and wounded hearts to be healed.

After decades of pastoring I have come to the conclusion that the initial relationships we have with our parents establish the types and ways we will relate with people for the rest of our lives. Therefore, within this chapter I want to share some thoughts with both parents and children however old they might be. Age may add perspective and wisdom, but it doesn't always bring healing. Yet there is still time to love well.

It's easy to take a shot at other parents for the way they raise their children. You're in the supermarket and a little boy is disobeying his mother, refusing to stop grabbing items and screaming at the top of his lungs when she tries to correct him. Or you notice a brother and sister fighting over what seems like nothing as you stroll through Macy's. Something in you wants to judge the parenting skills, and yet something else in you is a little relieved. Why? Because you realize that you're not the only parent who has to deal with kids, stores, and screams.

Parenting is not an easy job. Even with all the amazing resources out there today, success is not guaranteed. However, we can determine to live righteously in our homes and cultivate an atmosphere of love.

Knowing the difference between right and wrong in itself does not transform a child. That's a great start and please don't skip that lifelong lesson. But if the home is a place of pain and confusion, lessons of right become lessons of judgment, and lessons of wrong become yelling sessions that model and teach further abuse, both verbal and physical.

The greatest lessons are caught, not taught.

Children will obey out of fear but will then model the same patterns in the years to come. That cycle can be broken, but it takes a broken person to do it.

> Hurt people hurt people,
> but healed people heal people.

Just like alcohol addiction is often passed through multiple generations, so too are patterns of anger, mistrust, jealously, and violence. Thank God that He holds the keys to our liberty.

(If you are a parent, please don't read this chapter as

a judgment of your parenting ability. I am a parent, and there wasn't a day when my kids were little that I wasn't convinced that I was probably doing irreparable harm to them because of my imperfect parenting. The parents who are convinced everything they do is right are the ones who scare me.)

If a child's home is safe, it becomes a place of laughter and learning. If the home is filled with anxiety and fear, the biggest lessons learned are those of survival. Survival teaches people to look out for themselves. Lessons learned within an atmosphere of love teach people how to see and care for others.

When I say *safe*, I don't mean a home that lacks discipline. A lack of discipline does not equate to safety. Proverbs 15:10 says that "he who hates correction will die." It's not good to live apart from correction or discipline. Hebrews 12:11 assures us that, though no chastening seems joyful for the moment, those who give themselves to godly discipline will yield the "peaceable fruit of righteousness." What a great promise!

If the atmosphere of the home is rooted in love and respect, children will understand the discipline that is directed their way. Oh, they'll whine and cry at the moment, but in the end they will see the parent's heart. And with the knowledge that they are loved, they will move on, absorbing in their little hearts lessons that will bring forth peaceable fruit in the days ahead.

Every parent looks for that "peaceable fruit." A wise man and good friend of mine, Russ Merwin (father of six wonderful girls), said it well:

> A culture of love in a home comes by a parent's understanding of each child as a unique human being, with gifts hidden within, waiting to be watered and nurtured. Modeling a consistent and loving lifestyle will allow children to grow into who they were meant to be. When parents are involved and paying attention to their children, to the point where they recognize their talents, even naming them and encouraging them out loud, and then giving them opportunities and experiences for those talents to develop, those children will be able to enter into life with a huge advantage. Such children have direction and courage.

The out-loud encouragement Russ mentions here has a name. It's called a parental blessing.

As parents we are to lead. We are to set the example for our homes. But a few questions for the kids to answer might not be a bad idea. Questions such as "Is home a safe place for you? Do you feel noticed and encouraged here?

What are some of your dreams and how can I help you move toward them?"

When my kids were little, I used their sense of family and togetherness as a barometer to reveal how much ministry or travel was good for me. They did not lead me or own me, yet knowing their hearts was a huge part of how I made decisions about how often I worked late or went on the road. I was the dad, and there was no question about that. But even when they were little, it was important to me for them to have input in our home and the direction of our family. Not every decision was unanimous, but they all felt that as a family, we moved as one, as opposed to dad the dictator leading his little flock of minions.

As a parent, being present has no replacement. Conversely, being home all the time is no guarantee that you are preparing your children well.

You can come home from work early and spend every weekend at home, but if you are disconnected from your children emotionally, that's not much different from being gone all the time.

For some kids, what happens in the home reinforces that they are unimportant to their parents. Then someone comes along and tells them how lovely and needed they are. All too often it's the wrong person doing the kind of encouraging that the parents should have been doing in the first place.

I was in an Asian country recently, and a man introduced me to his daughter, a lovely girl in her mid-teens with a beautiful smile. When I said, "You have a beautiful daughter," he said, "Oh my, I never tell her that." I'd heard that response many times, so I knew what was coming. He added, "If I told her she was beautiful, she would get a big head." I asked him if he thought she was beautiful, and he reluctantly said yes. The young girl immediately lit up.

I took him aside and said, "Your daughter truly is a beautiful young lady. And the person who convinces her of that the most will be the one she listens to and follows. Do you want that to be you? Or do you want that to be a seventeen-year-old boy who is after more than just giving her a compliment?"

He gazed at me with an awkward look. A moment later his expression transformed into an awakened awareness. He immediately went to his daughter and told her how wonderful and beautiful she was. She was radiant, and they embraced sweetly.

> Tell your children often that they are loved.
> And tell them why.

Parents, I'm not trying to give you a list of dos and don'ts as much as I'm attempting to communicate the importance of creating an atmosphere within the home that promotes honesty, highlights kindness, and encourages love.

Eat together and talk about the day. Some friends of mine have everyone share a "thumbs up" and a "thumbs down" during dinner. Each member of the family is free to discuss a frustration he or she experienced during the day as well as talk about something positive that happened that day. Both expressions within a supportive and loving atmosphere are necessary for children to process at home. Better there, with you taking advantage of gentle teaching moments, than elsewhere, with a peer who lacks wisdom and doesn't have your child's best interest in mind.

You have probably heard the expression "tough love." Real love often has to be tough in order to raise a child's basic standard of conduct. If done rightly, though, tough love is not toughest on the child but on the parent. Maintaining an acceptable level of conduct is not an easy task. Children, like water, will often move toward the lowest level. And they usually remain there until another standard is modeled, taught, and enforced.

> That's why tough love is toughest on the parents.
> But love will find a way to make it happen.

But "tough love" doesn't mean "harsh love." Remember not to compare your children or their behavior with other children from other homes. That is dangerous and never ends well. But it's easy to see the weaknesses of our children and miss their innate strengths. And after a while, we become the parent we never wanted to be. When we feel "less than," we pull back from others out of self-judgment and shame.

Some parents are all too happy to share with you their latest parenting tips. They see a weakness in one of your children and *wham*, you're blasted with their latest teaching or most recent success. If you're a parent, please don't do that. Most likely you won't be fully heard, and there's a chance you'll be abhorred. It's better to hold your peace until you're asked.

That said, it is good to go to people you respect and ask them to share with you their thoughts on parenting. It takes a humble heart, but those who seek after wisdom are wise. As Proverbs 3:13 says, "Happy is the man who finds wisdom, and the man who gains understanding." Wouldn't you rather humble yourself, learn something from others, and be happier?

As parents we are to turn our hearts toward our children. But children are also to turn their hearts toward their parents. I realize that children will probably not be reading this book, but no matter our age, we are still children and we can all learn how to become more respectful and honoring to the mothers and fathers in our lives, whether they be biological or spiritual.

Having an abusive father did not create within me a loving heart. I hated him for hurting me and for his cruel words. But when I began to follow Jesus at age nineteen, I felt within me a voice asking me what I should do about my father. I knew it was God asking me to forgive him and try to build a bridge to his heart.

It took a long time to get there, but eventually I did. Part of it was my journey of maturing as a man and part of it was my own needed healing. One major aspect of all this was the understanding that I couldn't change his heart but I can change mine. That was my first step, and God knew exactly what I needed. I had an encounter with God that showed me the depth of His love for me. It was personal and intimate, and it empowered me to give my father the gift of forgiveness. You can read more about that amazing encounter in my book *The Wild Love of God*.

Even during the difficult years, I learned one important lesson: blessing comes when we honor our parents. One of the Ten Commandments reads, "Honor your father and your mother, that your days may be long upon the land" (Exodus 20:12). This commandment is not just for small children. We need to instill within our children the importance of being respectful and obedient to their parents and to those God has given as authorities in their lives. But we need to carry this truth in our hearts for our entire lives.

"Yes, sir" and "No, ma'am" are not outdated forms of communication. You can use those words to show honor and appreciation to those who are in your world and in your sphere of influence.

If I learn how to be an honoring son, I will hopefully grow into the kind of man who loves his children well and produces children who honor others as well. As Genesis 1:24 says, each form of God's creation produced others "according to its own kind." That cycle has been in effect, not just in the plant and animal world, but also in the heart and integrity of parents and leaders. We pass on what and who we are.

We have the capacity to carry on a legacy that can pass negativity and discord to another generation, or we can inspire another generation to love with the love that they've been given and to use their lives as a channel of God's grace and mercy. Our choices now will make all the difference in our life now and in the lives of future generations.

My Love Project

Your children are watching you more than you realize. If you want to influence your children's future, be available and influence their present. Schedule time this week to spend time engaged with your children, setting an atmosphere of love in your home. It is true that children are not a distraction from more important work. They are *the most* important work.[23]

10

TAKE THIS JOB
AND LOVE IT

A disappointing sports injury in high school caused me to lose some athletic scholarships, which led to my going to a nearby community college. Each day presented me with a new reason to party, and I took advantage of it. By the end of my first year of college, I was basically bottoming out. I returned to my mother's house for the summer, hoping to figure out how I was going to survive another year.

Shortly after I got home, I received a call from a former high school classmate. She and her father ran one of two dairy farms in the town. Her dad's health had taken a turn for the worse and she asked if I would be interested in helping them out by working alongside him for a week and then taking over his job for a while. I was very close to her and her family, so I said yes. I was happy to help them out and also earn some money during the summer months.

I had an abrupt wake-up call the next morning when my friend's father banged on the window outside my bedroom door at four o'clock and strongly encouraged me to get up and get going. I was out of the house in a flash. Unfortunately, I was pretty burned out from the night before.

People in Marion had been getting milk from this dairy for decades, and they expected it to arrive at their houses in time for breakfast. I, on the other hand, was used to sleeping till almost noon. I soon realized that I was going to have to change a few things in my life if I was going to do this job. I couldn't hang out with friends until two a.m. and do whatever I pleased. I was now a responsible adult…kinda.

It took a couple of weeks, but I soon started getting up at four and managed to develop a certain rhythm for the week. Monday, Wednesday, and Friday I delivered milk to homes, and Tuesday and Thursday I received a truckload of new milk and ran it through the pasteurizer. I ended those days by cleaning the big vat and the pipes that had heated and separated the milk.

It was hard work, but I was learning an important life lesson: when people rely on you for something, you are no longer the center of the universe.

I couldn't let down my town, but more important, I couldn't let down my friend and her family, especially during a time of pain and adversity. I knew I had a life-changing opportunity before me…if I would embrace it.

I later learned that my best friend's father, who had known me for years, told his son that he didn't think I could do it. He was sure the rigorous schedule would be too much for me.

Looking back now, I am grateful that I had that opportunity to work at the dairy. That job helped save my life. It pulled me out of some horrible habits. From sleeping too late to wasting time, I was on my way to a regrettable future. Being the milkman in Marion, New York, is something I will never regret.

Work is something we all have to do if we're going to eat and have clothes on our backs. And I have done myriad jobs over the years to put food on the table and a roof over my head. I've managed a bookstore, ordered medical supplies for a hospital, delivered furniture, been a bank teller, cut hair, been a salesman in New York City, worked in a health spa, worked as a surgical technician, taught junior high school, and been a real estate agent. During most of that time, I was the worship leader at my local church as well as one of the pastors. Just listing those tasks makes me tired! And I even left some things off the list.

To some it may sound as if I don't know who I am or what I'm doing. Actually, the opposite is true. It's because I know who I am that I have been able to do just about anything that has been put in front of me. Because my identity is not in what I do but in who I am, I am free to do anything. And because I am free to do most any kind of work, I can throw myself into my job and find ways to make that part of my life something meaningful as well as joyful.

I am loved by God. Fully! He doesn't love in part; He loves completely. Because my initial identity is as a beloved son, my day-to-day job does not own me or box me in, not in any way. I am free to be me. And that frees me to do whatever lies before me.

That freedom allows me to embrace the message found in Colossians 3:23, which says, "Whatever you do, do it heartily, as to the Lord and not to men." How liberating is that? I work for God. Yes, I have had a number of bosses over the years. But God is the Lord of lords, the King of kings, and the Boss of all bosses. He's always good!

I have met different kinds of people at my various jobs over the years. Some work strictly for the money. They hate what they do almost every minute they're doing it, and they don't mind telling you how they feel about their jobs and their bosses. I tend to stay clear of them, as they are always under a storm cloud and anyone who comes close to them will get wet, and possibly struck by the same kind of lightning that struck them. No, thanks. Fortunately, this group is a minority.

A second kind of employee is the one who absolutely loves his job. As a matter of fact, these people seem to be doing exactly what they were made for. They smile constantly and can't stop talking about how great a job they have.

In a church where I was an associate pastor, the children's pastor kept saying he had the greatest job in the world. One Sunday morning, I took off from my usual duties and joined him with the kids. Oh my, I love kids, but I was not made for that job. He, on the other hand, breezed through the morning, calling out each child by name, encouraging them while teaching them all at the same time. It was amazing. After we finished up that morning, he thanked me for coming in and went on and on about how great it was to have me there that day. After telling him it had been my pleasure, I turned around and asked God to forgive me for lying. Then I went home, threw myself on the couch, turned on a golf game, and promptly fell asleep.

People who combine their jobs with their greatest heart desires seem to have it all. To desire an occupation, and then get a chance to do something you love for a living, is a rare thing. To combine your vocation with your avocation is a gift, but it doesn't seem to be the norm.

A third type of worker is the workaholic. To some, the idea of being known as a workaholic is a compliment. They believe that working themselves to death is some kind of status symbol. They view themselves as dynamic, energetic, vigorous, and indestructible.

If you suffer from the belief that you need to burn the candle at both ends to make life work, please take a step back and rethink things. Did God put you on this earth to work? Second Thessalonians 3:10 says, "if anyone will not work, neither shall he eat," but that is pure and simple wisdom. It is not an invitation to work yourself to death. No one will stand before God and say, "Please send me back down, Lord, so I can work for a few more years."

Work is noble and it is part of life, but we are here to be loved and to love well. Our place of employment is a gift from God and an opportunity to express His heart through our words and our actions.

Our words will mean very little to people if our actions are contrary to what we say. If we talk about a God of love and are impatient with our bosses or coworkers, our words will fall to the ground like rocks.

I can say more through how I act than by what I say. My words take on more weight when they have been rightly introduced by kindness, love, and encouragement.

There is also a group of people who have embraced a sense of entitlement, which puts them in the opposite category of the workaholic. For some reason, these people have bought into the concept that they should be taken care of by someone else. We used to call such folks lazy, but that's not politically correct anymore.

If you feel like you deserve to be taken care of, you'd better stop, drop, and roll, because you have lit a fire that will eventually burn up everything around you. This is where 2 Thessalonians 3:10 comes into play. No workie—no eatie.

I understand the need for some people to receive help from outside sources while they try to land on their feet. I grew up with a single mom, after all. But somehow she made life happen. We didn't have a lot, but she never let us kids feel as if we were poor.

The last group of workers I've seen over the years is the group in which most people find themselves. They have acquired a job and begun to carve out a place of security and comfort within their role. They see themselves in two separate worlds. They work at one place and come home to another place.

There's nothing innately wrong with this picture unless the place you're at physically, whether home or work, is what forms your identity. In other words, when you're at work, you are an employee. When you're at home, you are a husband and father, or a wife and mother.

Yes, we all have roles in life. The problem comes when we lose our wholeness as individuals and live lives of compartmentalism. I do not lose my role as a husband just because I work away from home.

I made the opposite mistake when my kids were little. I started work very early most mornings, so I was able to head home at 3:20 p.m. Many days, I could have worked a little later and really helped out my workplace. Instead I played the "father to little kids card" and rarely made myself available for overtime. As I look back now, I wish I would have taken the opportunity to work an hour longer one or two days a week. I could have modeled my faith much more by being a more relied-upon employee.

It's sometimes a balancing act when you have things pulling at you from every direction. What has helped me is the knowledge that I am not my own. It took me a while to realize that no one but God owns me, and because of that, anyone can steer me at my work if God has put me there.

Remember Joseph from the Old Testament? After being greatly honored by his father, he found himself at the mercy of his angry brothers, almost dying at their hands. He was then carted off to live as a slave, yet he knew who he was and managed to surmount every obstacle. He went from being a slave to leading a household. Then he was once again thrown under the bus (or in this case, the chariot). This time he was worse than a slave; he was a prisoner. Yet even then, he rose to the top—not by complaining, but by showing who he was: a man loved and led by God, full of integrity, who could be trusted by prisoner and guard alike.

It is easy to see yourself as a worker one minute and a

husband the next, a cog in the wheel one minute and a loving father the next. Instead of allowing the place you're at to define who you are, let God define you. When He does, you will rise above the pettiness that overwhelms so many at their workplaces.

I am a beloved son who sometimes teaches junior high kids. I am a beloved son who has helped people buy new homes. I am a beloved son who gets to preach every now and then. All of these roles and responsibilities are wonderful, yet none of them defines me...because I am a beloved son.

> What would happen if people let God define who they are and then took that secured identity and carried His love and affection wherever they went?

What would happen if we were able to not just survive our workdays but to flourish during our time at work?

I'm not saying we have to deeply love everything about our jobs. But when we are convinced that we are loved, we can take that root of loving security wherever we go. We no longer live to be validated; we actually live to help validate others.

A workplace expression of love will look very different from how we express love at home or in church. But we can love well wherever we are. If you find it hard to even think about loving your job, replace the word *love* with something that better expresses God's heart for those you work with. Instead of looking for someone to praise you for your efforts or applaud you for all your hard work, become the one who comes to work prepared to give others the thing you desire most: encouragement.

A friend once told me that after he encouraged a coworker one day, she told him, "If my husband would have given me a compliment like that, even just every once in a while, we'd probably still be married."

> There is a deficit of genuine, life-giving encouragement in our workplaces today. We can fill that gap.

You will not regret living a life of encouragement. On the contrary, you will get back much more than you could ever give out. So arm yourself with words that inspire and refresh people. If you do, you too will become inspired and refreshed. Prepare yourself to energize the tired people around you and champion those who work in the shadows and need someone to notice them. When you do these things, you too will be energized and blessed…beyond imagination.

I know some people who love what they do and would never even think of leaving their jobs for a few more bucks. I live in Nashville and am surrounded by all sorts of musicians. Sometimes the money is great; other times it's a struggle to pay the bills.

As Christians, we need to let God's wisdom direct our lives instead of allowing human desire to rule. This will bring about a greater understanding of what we're doing and how our work may affect others. We are not islands unto ourselves. Our decisions make a difference to other people.

If my pursuit of my dream job is killing my family, something isn't right. There is always a way out, but it may require me to lay some things down in exchange for something more important.

Work is a gift from God. But not everyone who wants a job has one. If you do, I encourage you to remember the following:

- "Whatever you do, do it heartily, as to the Lord" (Colossians 3:23).
- Jesus came to give us abundant life, not abundant work. Don't let your employment own you; you own it.
- Let your workplace become a field where you are able to plant seeds of appreciation and encouragement.
- Let your life speak louder than your words. But as Colossians 4:6 says, "Let your speech always be with grace, seasoned with salt, that you know how you ought to answer everyone." This is not

a call to talk; it's a call to speak with kindness and wisdom.

- Don't feel guilty if you don't love your job. Being faithful until God leads you elsewhere is vitally important in a world of limited commitments.
- Keep your heart in a safe place. It's easy to find fault with people and systems where you work. As Philippians 2:14 says, "Do all things without complaining and disputing." Following this wise word will save you many hassles and heartaches.

Let God, not what you do, define who you are. If you see yourself only as a servant, then God is merely a Master. Remember, He's also a Father, and we are His loved ones! Learn to be loved so that you can love others...even at work.

My Love Project

Someone else can always do your job, but no one can do it like you can. Be a light where you work, but don't shine so brightly in someone's face that he or she has no choice but to turn away. Draw people in from the shadows. Today let one person know you appreciate him or her. Try it again tomorrow. Daily fill your world with simple words of encouragement.

11

LIVING LOVED

One of the great encouragers in the Bible was a man named Joses. You may know him as Barnabas. He went on the road with the apostle Paul, but there was much more to Barnabas than just being Paul's tagalong.

I first learned about Barnabas in 1973. I was nineteen years old, recently saved, and I ate up everything my older and wiser Bible teacher said. He talked about the apostolic team of Paul and Barnabas, and explained that through a series of unforeseen circumstances, Barnabas blew it and was never heard from in Scripture again.

Not knowing the full story at the time, I wondered, *Why did Paul choose Barnabas in the first place? There must have been something about him that Paul liked.* Yet my Bible teacher had very little good to say about Barnabas. He portrayed him as a man we should all strive not to be like.

Something about that didn't seem right to me. So I dug a little deeper into the Word to see what actually took place.

The introduction of Barnabas into Scripture almost reveals the whole story. In Acts 4, as the disciples were boldly sharing the word of God with great effectiveness and power, multitudes of believers began to gather and unite as one. People were selling their property and goods and allowing them to be distributed to all who were in need. One of those who came forward was a man called Joses, who sold his land and brought his money to the disciples so they could distribute it with wisdom.

He was apparently already known by the disciples, who changed his name—as was the custom in those days. He went from Joses, meaning, "May God give increase," to Barnabas, which means, "the son of encouragement." When those who know you best give you a name like that, you must have something good going on.

In Acts 9, when the newly converted Paul (known as Saul at the time) tried to connect with the disciples in Jerusalem, they turned him away. They didn't trust him because of his violent past. He was known throughout the land as being unafraid to harass and persecute believers, and had even been a party to the killing of members of the early church. Though they had heard about his conversion, Paul was not one of them. He was the enemy.

At this time, Barnabas got to know Paul, and he knew the

kind of man he had become since his dramatic conversion on the road to Damascus. Being the son of encouragement that he was, Barnabas took Paul to the disciples and captivated them with stories of Paul's conversion, his new life in Christ, and how God had used Paul through the power of his preaching.

Finally, the church leaders received Paul as one of their own, and his new life in the church began.

Now I knew the truth. Paul didn't choose Barnabas; Barnabas chose Paul!

Soon after, Barnabas found himself in another situation where he could encourage and befriend Paul. Because of the number of new believers coming to Christ in Antioch, the leaders in Jerusalem sent Barnabas out to teach, mentor, and disciple them.

After spending some time there, he saw the need to have another person by his side. Barnabas took a journey, seeking out Paul, who then returned with him to Antioch. Together, side by side, they ministered to the church and ushered in many new believers, most of them Gentiles.

They spent a year there, and it was in this place, at that time, that believers were first called Christians, meaning "followers of Christ." You don't get a label for nothing. Barnabas and Paul must have been amazing examples of the life and character of Jesus.

What did folks see in those two men that made the

people there call the followers of Jesus Christians? Others were also preaching powerfully, and miracles followed all the apostles as they traveled and ministered across the Middle East and beyond. But nowhere else were they called Christians. Only in Antioch. Why?

I don't believe it was just the signs and wonders, and I'm sure it was not the great oratory skills of either Paul or Barnabas. I believe it was a man who set an example, who shone as Jesus shone. Barnabas loved well, he forgave, he was tender, he believed in people, and he was a friend.

In our culture, friendship has taken a step back from what we call our Christian mandate. If we must follow God no matter the cost, people become a commodity, a tool to accomplish what God has directed us to do. When they become less productive or are no longer needed, they are easily discarded. Such was not the mind-set of Barnabas.

> Barnabas was committed to those around him, not just seeing their gifts but seeing their souls, their God-given value, their inherent worth.

He not only knew what they did, he knew who they were. When Barnabas and Paul next traveled to Jerusalem, they brought John Mark with them. Throughout Acts 13, 14, and 15, we read about their continued exploits as the Holy Spirit called Barnabas and Paul to partner together.

Paul and Barnabas were comrades in God's kingdom. This seemed a partnership for the ages.

But when Paul decided to return to some of the places where they had ministered, Barnabas mentioned that he wanted to take John Mark along for the journey. Paul remembered how John Mark had suddenly left them and returned home from their last trip together, and he didn't want the immature, homesick young man to tag along on their important apostolic journey.

The contention became so great that Paul and Barnabas severed ties. Paul teamed up with Silas, and Barnabas took John Mark and sailed to Cyprus.

Except for some informational comments made by Paul in the epistles, Barnabas is never heard from again in Scripture.

Years ago I heard about a church that had a chicken coup on their property. Some members of the congregation wanted to enlarge the coup, get chickens, sell the eggs, and make money for the church. Others wanted to tear down the old eyesore and use the land for better purposes. I'm sure you can guess what happened. The church split over what should be done with the chicken coup.

Though not as silly as a congregational breakup over a chicken coup, the breakup of Paul and Barnabas made me equally sad.

I was taught that Barnabas was a nice guy, but a

weakness in him prevented him from accomplishing what God had originally called him to do.

What was his weakness? Too much compassion and commitment to those around him? When my teacher told me that Barnabas' weakness was that he had a habit of putting people before the latest cause, I knew I liked Barnabas.

What happened to Barnabas after he and Paul went their separate ways? We don't learn the answer to that from what is written in Scripture. Instead, our knowledge of Barnabas' legacy is determined through his effect upon his young disciple, John Mark.

John Mark was the cousin of Barnabas, which probably explains his strong love and support of the young man. *Barnabas put family before ministry. What a concept!*

After leaving with Barnabas, John Mark became the leader of the church in Alexandria, Egypt, a model church that was a shining light to the entire region.

Though John Mark was a young man at the time when Jesus walked, he had firsthand knowledge of His life and also the lives of the disciples who surrounded Him. He took his experience and knowledge, and the love and encouragement he received from Barnabas, and wrote a book that multitudes have come to know and love.

The book was subsequently named after him, but he didn't use both his Roman name (Marcus) and his Jewish name (John). Only his Roman name was used as the title. We know the book as the gospel of Mark.

What happened with John Mark clearly displays the power that's found in the spirit of encouragement and real, live, practical love. A fearful young man was brought back to life and went on to become a pillar in the church, eventually writing one of the Gospels. I love it. God loves it too!

In the book of Colossians, Paul writes in the fourth (and final) chapter about a handful of people who had been his most loyal and faithful friends. They had stayed with him throughout his latest prison ordeal, and he said they "have proved to be a comfort to me." Included in that list is John Mark. He knew what it meant to be encouraged, and he in turn was an encouragement to others. May it be so with us!

As I travel around the world I am constantly amazed at the incredible people I meet: faithful, loving, servant-hearted folks. I am honored and humbled to call them my brothers and sisters in Christ and also to call them my friends.

Yet no matter where I go, all people—even those who appear strong on the outside and who seem to have it all together—need to know they're loved and that they have the support and encouragement of the community around them.

That's why, wherever I go, I always stop the instruction from time to time and tell people I love them, and *why* I love them. I call it my "I love you because" time. I sometimes ask one of the leaders if they know someone there who needs to be loved on or encouraged. I sometimes pick some folks I have seen who appear to need a supportive word. Often the selection seems random, yet God always has a purpose with each one chosen. If the group is small enough and there's time, I highlight each person present over the course of my time there.

These moments never pass without many hugs and tears. I've had spouses do this, and in a short time they are weeping in each other's arms, embracing in a new and special way. It's one thing to daily say to a spouse, "I love you." It's entirely different to explain why he or she means so much to you. Our ears, our hearts, our very spirits, long to hear why we are special to someone else.

I recently buried a friend after a long illness. A few months after that, another friend passed away very suddenly. Within two weeks of that, a third friend quietly left this world for his eternal home. Psalm 39:5 says that "certainly every man at his best state is but a vapor." If a vapor is the best we've got, we need to remember we're here for just a breath.

When we're young, we think we'll live forever. We won't.

> We have one life to live and to love well. Why not lavish that love on the people you know best?

Tell those who have stood with you over the years why they are special to you. Tell them what they mean to you. Give kindness to those who have shown you kindness, and let them know that you notice and appreciate the little things they do for you and for others. That will strengthen them to continue with those important acts of kindness.

Take it past the small circle of church and family. Stop using the drive-through at the bank and the fast-food places you visit regularly. Instead go inside and engage people face-to-face. They may not be able to talk long, but they will stop for a word of encouragement and thanks. You, and they, will never forget that moment, and you will never regret the extra time you spent.

I'm not talking about momentary acts of kindness. Those are good and I encourage that. But what I'm referring to here is being a light that shines God's life, light, and love to a world that is hungry for something real. Something powerful happens when love is progressively expressed to specific people over a period of time. We can each make a difference if we decide to be intentional with love.

Obviously we need to show discretion. I am not going to

give a gift to an individual female. I'm a married man, and the appearance of something inappropriate, even if done innocently, is wrong. I can, however, with the knowledge and support of my wife, create a lifestyle that allows me to bless those around me without creating inappropriate ties to people. Simple wisdom can go a long way.

Five intimidating mountains loom around us, trying to separate us from one another. Generational, gender, ethnic, economic, and religious differences don't just threaten to cage us in and keep us safe within our comfort zone; they work overtime to create animosity, jealousy, and contempt between each distinction.

Jesus warned his followers that the thief comes only to steal, kill, and destroy (John 10:10). Our enemy's work is to divide and conquer. He loves nothing more than to bring rancor and mistrust between old and young, men and women, black and white, and one religion from another.

> Whose voice will we listen to, and who will capture our hearts? Whoever gets our hearts gets our lives.

Will we answer to the one who wants to isolate and separate us, or to the one who brings abundant life? My dear friend Mike Bickle describes the battle for the human heart as a beauty contest. Whoever woos us wins and eventually becomes our master.

So how do we end this discussion on love? Well, hopefully we don't. No successful cultural transformation is achieved if the thoughts and ideals being expressed are just a momentary event. The American Revolution was not intended to be a single battle to express our dislike toward the throne of England. Its purpose was to bring radical change to our form of government and redefine what it meant to be an American.

God wants to redefine what it means to be His followers. As 1 John 4:8 says, God is love. Those who call themselves His followers must leave in their wake His thoughts, His heart, His tangible affection, His words, His example, and even His fragrance, wherever we go.

A quote attributed to William Gladstone, the former Prime Minister of England, is one of my favorites. It says, "We look forward to the time when the Power of Love will replace the Love of Power. Then will our world know the blessings of peace."[24]

I've heard it said many times that love is a verb. That's a cute saying, but the reality is, it's a biblical maxim. If you do an even cursory look at the word *love* in the New Testament, you will see that it is always connected to some type of outward expression. It's not just "God so loved the world that He gave." The new covenant is filled with invitations to love with action.

Faith without works is dead, but so is love without its

connected expression. Like a gourmet meal sitting on an exquisitely laid-out table hidden away in some faraway cave, so too are loving feelings hidden away within human hearts. They may make the caves of our hearts feel warmed, replete with delectable aromas, but if they remain locked away, no one benefits from the potential feast.

The world is waiting and the world is watching. There is war from one end of this earth to the other. Can we, in our own worlds, bring peace to those around us through how we live lives of demonstrated love? I think we can.

Not everyone can sing like a professional. Not everyone can afford a new car or house. Not everyone can repair a diseased heart. But we all have the capacity to love. With loved and healed hearts, we have the ability to help other hearts become whole.

> Love today. It's not too late. And when tomorrow comes, you'll have the whole day to find someone who needs love and encouragement.

The words may be "I appreciate you because…" Or they may come out as "I enjoy your company because…" But what we are actually saying, and what people are genuinely hearing, is "You are wanted and you are needed," which every heart needs to hear. "I love you because…" are powerful words!

Is it true that all you need is love? No. We need faith and we need hope. But as 1 Corinthians 13 says, "Now abide faith, hope and love, these three; but the greatest of these is love."

An old recruitment slogan for the Navy stated, "It's not a job, it's an adventure." The same can be said for The Love Project. It's not a job, it's a lifestyle. It's not work, it's fun. Whether at home, on the job, or somewhere in between, we are always called to love.

It's simple, really. As Jesus said in John 13:34–35, "A new commandment I give to you, that you love one another; as I have loved you. By this all will know that you are my disciples, if you have love for one another." Open your heart to God's love, and then go and do likewise, for the greatest thing we can ever do in this life is love well.

As Paul said to the Romans, "Let love be genuine. ... Love one another with brotherly affection. ... Outdo one another in showing honor" (Romans 12:9–10).

There are people all around you who are waiting for you to encourage them with words of life. They are longing for you to love them with intentional and practical expressions of affection.

May your life become a walking love project.

My Love Project

Don't let a day go by without letting someone know why he or she is loved or appreciated. Refuse to let the potential of tomorrow's blessing steal away the reality of blessing someone today. Today is the right day to love well.

12

LOVE PROJECT
CHALLENGE

During the summer of 2014, social media broadcasted thousands of people dumping buckets of ice and water on their heads. The Ice Bucket Challenge was a viral sensation and raised millions of dollars for the ALS cause. One charity reported that donations were fifty times what was normal. Truly revolutionary.

Today I encourage you to be a part of something even more revolutionary—something that can bring real change to your life and the lives of those around you. I jokingly considered calling it the Nice Bucket Challenge. But what I'd like to propose goes beyond dumping niceness on those around you—although that would be a good start. I'm inviting you to take part in the Love Project Challenge.

The Love Project Challenge is a natural extension of this

book's call to live a life of intentional love and encouragement with those you know and those you meet each day. As they say, actions speak louder than words. Beyond that, our actions give power to our words.

"I love you" and "I appreciate you" are powerful statements, but telling people *why* you love them or appreciate them goes much further.

So let's do that. Let's go beyond the norm. Let's build security in one another through uplifting, specific statements of love. And let's bring courage to one another through words and gifts of encouragement. Get good at finding the good in others, expressing that goodness in words that are honest and life giving to build up those who listen. Take the challenge to transform your world through daily intentional love and practical encouragement.

Level One

Level one has two challenges: a daily challenge and a yearly challenge.

1. **Daily challenge.** Every day, find three people to encourage with words of encouragement:
   » a family member
   » someone outside your family (e.g., a friend, neighbor, or coworker)

» a stranger (e.g., someone who serves you, like a waiter, cashier, flight attendant, or bus driver)

This challenge is simply to notice others—who they are and what they are doing well. You could say something like:

» You look great today.
» I love your smile.
» I appreciate your hard work.
» Your thoughtfulness is a real blessing.
» I love you because you take the time to listen to me.
» I'm thankful to be on your team because your insight has guided these important decisions.

Remember to attach a "because" statement to your encouragement. You don't always have to say the word *because*, but make sure the person knows something specific you love or appreciate.

2. **Yearly challenge.** Once a year, plan a "love intervention" or "encouragement ambush." Gather a small group of people at a home or place of business, each person armed with words of encouragement and love. Have each person look someone in the eye and say, "I love you because..."

and then finish the sentence. For some (especially in work environments) it will be more appropriate to say, "I appreciate you because…," which is fine. The most important part of the challenge is to say what needs to be said so that people can hear what needs to be heard. At the end of the event, encourage each participant to do the same for another person in his or her life within two months. (Optional extra: bring small gifts for the person—nothing expensive, but tokens that speak of relationship, filled with warmth and sentiment.)

Level Two

Level two has three challenges: both challenges of level one (see above) plus a monthly challenge.

3. **Monthly challenge.** Write an encouraging note or buy a small gift for one of the people in your life who serves you (e.g., postal worker, waste remover, bank teller, teacher, manager, bus driver, clergy).

Level Three

Level three has four challenges: the three challenges of levels one and two (see above) plus a challenge to share the event with others.

4. **Record and remember.** Record (video or audio) yourself or a group doing a love intervention or encouragement ambush (see level one), then give the recording to the person to remember the event.

Share Your Love Project Challenge

Please share any of these love project challenges at

www.loveprojectchallenge.com

or (with permission from the one you are encouraging) post to social media with the tag #loveprojectchallenge.

I believe we can transform the world through intentional love and practical encouragement. But even if we don't reach that goal in our lifetime, I'm certain we can bring positive change to many people as we receive God's everlasting love daily and find practical, meaningful ways to give it away.

Be loved, take the challenge, and love well.

Acknowledgments

F irst and foremost I want to thank my wife, children, and grandkids for enlarging my heart and deepening my capacity to love. You have all shown me great love and appreciation over the years, and its effect means the world to me. You are my greatest gifts from God. I love you so much!

To my brother, Mark. Thank you for being my brother as well as my friend. Your ongoing support has sustained me, especially when I've walked through the shadowy places. I love you. You're like family.

To David Sluka, who has been a rock throughout this whole process. Your patience and vision for me and this book has been an incredible blessing. Thank you for believing in me, not just with your words, but with your heart and actions. I hope there are many more collaborations out there in the future. You're a great man.

Carlton Garborg, a big thank-you for hearing my thoughts and ideas and actually thinking that there was a book hidden in there somewhere. Your spirit of excellence has helped encourage me to rise to the occasion. Thank you for this wonderful opportunity to partner with you and BroadStreet Publishing. I'm honored.

And last, but certainly not least, thanks go out to my buddy Paul Rogers for seeing years ago that there were words locked somewhere in my mind. It's a little scary inside there, but you ventured in and pulled out the writer in me. I will be forever grateful for that, and also for your amazing friendship.

Endnotes

1   Patty Onderko, "The New Science of Mother-Baby Bonding," Parenting .com, © Copyright 2014, Meredith Corporation, www.parenting.com/ article/the-new-science-of-mother-baby-bonding, accessed Oct. 7, 2014.

2   Arlene Harris, "A mother's love for her baby may be based on smell," IrishExaminer.com, Feb. 2, 2014, www.irishexaminer.com/lifestyle/ healthandlife/parenting/a-mothers-love-for-her-baby-may-be-based-on-smell-256995.html, accessed Oct. 7, 2014.

3   Ibid.

4   Benedict Carey, "Addicted to Mother's Love: It's Biology, Stupid," *The New York Times* online news, June 29, 2004, www.nytimes. com/2004/06/29/health/psychology/29bond.html accessed Oct. 7, 2014.

5   www.divorcestatistics.org summarizes these and other divorce statistics from a variety of reputable sources.

6   "Study shows couples who live together before engagement are more likely to struggle," *University of Denver Magazine* online news, July 15, 2009, http://magazine.du.edu/academics-research/ study-shows-couples-who-live-together-before-engagement-are-more-likely-to-struggle/, accessed Oct. 7, 2014.

7   Anup Shah, "Today, around 21,000 children died around the world," Sept. 24, 2001, http://www.globalissues.org/article/715/today-21000-children-died-around-the-world, accessed Oct. 7, 2014.

8   There are a number of resources that confirm these numbers, including Walk Free Global Slavery Index 2013 - www.globalslaveryindex. org/findings/?gclid=CMaq08Tq5LoCFS4aOgod_AoALA#overview; https://www.freetheslaves.net/document.doc?id=34; and http://borgen-project.org/10-statistics-on-slavery-today/.

9   Prof. Robert E. Black, MD, et al., "Maternal and child undernutrition and overweight in low-income and middle-income countries," *The Lancet*, Volume 382, Issue 9890, Pages 427–451, 3 August 2013, http://www.thelancet.com/journals/lancet/article/PIIS0140-6736(13)60937-X/fulltext, accessed Oct. 7, 2014.

10 Roger Ebert, "Love Story (Review)," Jan. 1, 1970, www.rogerebert.com/reviews/love-story-1970. Ebert Digital. Retrieved 2014-03-11.

11 From the movie *Love Story*, by Erich Segal.

12 Stephanie Sample, email message to David Sluka as edited from her Facebook post Sept. 30, 2014, used by permission.

13 A summary of a true story by Christy Claassen, "A Helping Hand of Applause - Kindness of Strangers," www.readersdigest.com.au/ks-a-helping-hand-of-applause, accessed July 6, 2014.

14 Names have been changed.

15 Stress in America, American Psychological Association, www.apa.org/news/press/releases/stress/2012/full-report.pdf.

16 D. Umberson, J. K. Montez, "Social Relationships and Health: a Flashpoint for Health Policy," *Journal of Health & Social Behavior*, 2010; 51 Suppl:S54-66, Department of Sociology, University of Texas, Austin, TX, http://www.ncbi.nlm.nih.gov/pmc/articles/PMC3150158.

17 Dr. Carolyn Leaf, "The Science of Love," September 29, 2011, http://drleaf.com/blog/the-science-of-love/, accessed Oct. 1, 2014.

18 Kory Floyd, Alan C. Mikkelson, Colin Hesse, Perry M. Pauley, "Human Communication Research," v33 n2, April 2007, 119–142.

19 K. C. Light, K. M. Grewen, J. A. Amico, "Biological Psychology," Department of Psychiatry, University of North Carolina, Chapel Hill, NC, 69(1):5–21, April 2005.

20 Tracie White, "Love takes up where pain leaves off, brain study shows," Oct. 13, 2010, http://med.stanford.edu/news/all-news/2010/10/love-takes-up-where-pain-leaves-off-brain-study-shows.html, accessed Oct. 9, 2014.

21 J. A. Coan, H. S. Schaefer, R. J. Davidson, Department of Psychology, University of Virginia, Charlottesville, VA. "Psychological Science,"17(12):1032–9, December 2006.

22 "Millennials in Adulthood," Pew Research Social and Demographic Trends, March 7, 2014, http://www.pewsocialtrends.org/2014/03/07/millennials-in-adulthood, accessed Oct. 8, 2014.

23 These words are attributed to both C. S. Lewis and John Trainer, MD.

24 Attributed in *The Forbes Book of Business Quotations* (1997) edited by Edward C. Goodman and Ted Goodman, p. 639. Also see http://en.wikiquote.org/wiki/William_Ewart_Gladstone.